SMOKEHOUSE BEAR

SMOKEHOUSE BEAR

More Alaskan Recipes and Stories

From the Author of Lowbush Moose
Gordon R. Nelson

ALASKA NORTHWEST PUBLISHING COMPANY
Anchorage, Alaska

Library of Congress cataloging in publication data:
Nelson, Gordon R., 1922-
    Smokehouse bear.
    Includes index.
    1. Cookery, American—Alaska. I. Title.
TX715.N43 1982   641.5   82-1743
ISBN 0-88240-227-7   AACR2

Cover and some illustrations by Val Paul Taylor
Design and some illustrations by Cathy Cullinane

Alaska Northwest Publishing Company
Box 4-EEE, Anchorage, Alaska 99509

Printed in U.S.A.

To Alaskans and other Americans
who may either visit or join us in the Great Land:
Let us grow with care, remembering the people of
the past and the future.

CONTENTS

CHOOSING A TITLE

CHAPTER 1

Why title this book *SMOKEHOUSE BEAR?* No doubt a title is necessary, and it should be at least suggestive of the contents. So take your choice of the following reasons.

There may be a recipe for smoked bear within these covers. I remember eating off of a smoke-cured ham a number of years ago up at Caribou Creek on the Glenn Highway, when Ben Hitchcock invited me in for lunch one day.

He brought to the table a large bear ham and plunked it down on a board between us. He reached across and handed me the butt end of a hunting knife. "Slice it thin for the best taste," he advised.

I made a good meal out of smoked bear ham, homemade bread and beer. At times I can still taste it. I quickly jotted down a few notes on how Ben cured the ham.

He had caught the black bear in a favorite blueberry patch up the mountain. He dispatched the bear and reduced the carcass to loads he could carry home in several trips. The two hams he saved for the last load and on the way home remembered the smokehouse was already at work curing the winter's salmon. His mind shifted directly to smoked bear.

Just outside the smokehouse was a twenty-gallon crock that he used to brine pieces of salmon before smoking them. It was empty, so Ben dropped in the two bear hams and added his favorite marinade: salt and brown sugar, two handfuls of the former and one of the latter, for each gallon of water needed to cover the meat.

Two days later he hung the hams in the back corner of the smokehouse and forgot about them. He went on smoking salmon for another three weeks. On the day the smokehouse was shut down, he hung one ham in the cache and put the other one in the cooler beside the cabin. I arrived a week later.

I gave the ham my seal of approval by banging the handle of the knife on the top and slicing off three more thin slices. It sure made beer taste good.

Incidentally, you were just provided the only recipe for smoked bear you'll find in this book.

But back to the reasons for the title. It might also have been chosen to remind you that I wore a Smoky Bear hat for twenty-one years of my life. After all, his hat, in blue rather than forest green, is the official headgear of the Alaska State Troopers. And it was my travels as a trooper that gave me access to many of the recipes you will find in these pages.

There could be still a third reason for the title. When you add *SMOKEHOUSE BEAR* to your bookshelf, right beside my first cookbook, *LOWBUSH MOOSE*, your visitors will surely think you are an animal lover. I know I certainly am. I love a good steak, stew, meat loaf, meatballs and even barbecued liver.

Whatever the reason, it was a definite relief when I arrived at a title for my new book. I could then discuss the manuscript with my friends using a title. No longer was Nelson writing simply "another book." Nor did I stress the fact that it was "another cookbook." I just mentioned the title casually and let them come to their own conclusions.

With a title in hand, I could also mention that I'm "about to have another book published." That's quite an attention-getter. The ladies always seem to be interested in writers. Especially in published writers, known as *authors*. That's me, *AUTHOR*.

If the truth be known, the men are

FAMILY TABLE WINE

Your first requirement is to have something in which to ferment the wine. Most winemaking supply shops have an assortment of containers. I prefer the 5-gallon glass carboy. To this you will have to add a cork drilled for a bubbler. Later you will need a siphon to remove the wine without disturbing the settled dregs. For most everything else, your regular kitchen tools will do fine.

While you're in the winemakers' shop look at the cans and jugs of concentrated juices especially packaged for winemaking. If you are wealthy, go ahead and buy one to try.

My favorite place to obtain the juice necessary to make wine is the grocery store. For years I have used frozen grape concentrate for my table wine. But I caution you to check the contents of the concentrate carefully. You want cans that contain *only grapes and sugar.* Many producers are now cutting corners and adding artificial sweeteners which will not ferment and make alcohol. Luckily, you will still find some usable brands.

You will need:

9 pounds granulated sugar,
inverted as directed
2 tablespoons lemon juice
concentrate
5 12-ounce cans frozen grape
concentrate
Water to fill carboy as directed

1 package all-purpose wine yeast
(from a winemakers' shop)
2-1/2 teaspoons yeast nutrient
(buy at same shop)

First, invert the sugar by bringing 4 quarts of water to a boil in an 8-quart aluminum, stainless steel or enameled pot. Add the sugar and, when it dissolves, add the 2 tablespoons of lemon juice concentrate. Continue to simmer for 20 minutes. Cool the inverted sugar.

Let the frozen grape concentrate thaw while the sugar is cooling. Then combine the grape juice, inverted sugar, and enough water to fill the glass carboy to 5 inches from its top. Place the bubbler in the cork and seal the carboy. Let it stand for 24 hours to reach room temperature. Then add yeast and yeast nutrient. Gently shake the carboy.

The next ingredient is patience. Leave the carboy at room temperature, 65° to 75°, for a month.

I test mine with an alcohol tester and expect it to reach 13 percent by volume. Extend your waiting time until the desired percentage is reached. Then place the carboy in a very cool place and let the wine settle as long as you can wait.

Once it clears, it can be bottled. But try a little and place a bottle in the refrigerator. Give the rest of it at least 4 months and up to a year to age and mellow.

Remember to start a new batch as soon as the carboy is empty.

interested, too. They look upon male authors with some pride. For deep inside each man is the real and sensitive story of his struggle to reach his position in life, or the analysis of why he didn't reach his goals in life. In the rare case where success or failure is not his prime concern, the man is sure that he could write an educational book that would rival Chapman's or Kinsey's work in the field of sexual experience.

These men all know that if *he* can write a book, they, too, can achieve the same goal. That may be the cause of the faint smiles I have seen nearly every day since I became an *AUTHOR.*

Only one person I know wasn't impressed by my elevation to the status of author — my high school English teacher. It was reported to me that she said, "Write a book? Don't be silly! I still don't understand how he graduated from high school."

So take cheer all you would-be writers. If *he* can do it, so can you!

There is another way to make a hit at a gathering of friends: serve homemade wine. I have some coffee friends, some bourbon friends and some wine friends, but it's the latter who know me as the life of the party. Winemaking is one of my hobbies. It is, after all, just another way of preserving food.

Yes, I know you could make jams and jellies out of the same grapes and berries, but can you imagine me moving through a crowd in my living room dropping spoonfuls of strawberry jam into the guests' glasses? Should I add, "Peanut butter and jelly sandwich, anyone?"

I thought not, too. I choose to make wine out of the available. It's a hobby not

WINE CELLAR SANGRIA

When one develops a wine cellar, be it 5 bottles or 500, it becomes possible to think of wine as a summertime cooler. So it is with us, and we serve the following:

1 cup water
1 cup sugar
1 cup orange juice
1 fresh lime, sliced (or 2 table-
*   spoons lime juice)*
1 cup strawberries, fresh or frozen
1/2 cup brandy (optional)
1 fifth white wine, chilled from the
*   cellar*
1 fresh orange, sliced in eighths

In a large pitcher combine the water and sugar. Stir until sugar is dissolved. Add the orange juice, lime, strawberries, and brandy, if used. This mixture should stand for 2 hours in the refrigerator to blend the flavors.

Just before serving, add the cool wine and gently stir. Place an orange slice in a wine glass and fill with Sangria. Serve with pride.

without its ups and downs, so to speak. On its way to making me a hit, it came near ruining a good marriage. My own!

Once, through a fluke in processing, I created a case of nice, sparkling red wine. When a group of friends dropped in, I went to the cellar to retrieve some for a treat. I returned with three bottles. Two of them I set on the kitchen counter. The third I opened to pour and serve in the living room.

I was on my feet again, pouring a second round into the glass of a lady wearing a white dress, when there was a loud "Blam!" from the kitchen. I looked up to see what had happened and poured half a glass of wine in the lady's lap.

Ignoring her screams, I ran to the kitchen, not to cover my embarrassment, but to save my kitchen. One of the remaining bottles had just exploded, reducing itself to a pile of broken glass and a puddle of wine, which was running across the counter and dripping onto the floor. Perhaps this would also be the time to mention my new splatter wallpaper design in wine red.

With the speed of a striking snake, I lifted the second bottle of wine from the ooze and shattered glass and set it across the kitchen on another counter. As I cleaned up the mess, a female guest joined me to help. She slipped and went to her pretty knees in wine. They were soon dripping red. I sincerely hoped with wine rather than blood.

Ten minutes later everything was under control except for Connie, my very disturbed wife, and an angry guest in a once-white dress, who had joined the group in the kitchen to express some unflattering opinions about my wine-pouring ability. She even hinted at some unkind suspicions about my parentage.

Suddenly the third bottle of wine suicided into this scene with a loud "Blam!" The pressure of the warming wine gases had proved too much for the bottle. I stood there in my splatter-patterned white shirt, maybe even wounded by flying glass, and reviewed all the nasty expressions I'd like to use.

Only a microsecond later the first of the giggles started. They expanded into full-blown laughter in another flick of time. The lady in once-white, the one in the red knees and my wife were laughing their darn fool heads off.

The lady in red and white said, "Gordy, you deserved that!"

While not agreeing with her, I couldn't keep my own sense of humor from coming to the fore. I even smiled a bit when I discovered I wasn't bleeding.

I returned to the cellar for three more bottles of wine, opened them all right away, and the party went on. The women giggled a lot, but we didn't waste another drop of wine.

Not all wine has to be bubbly, or even aged, to be good. The prime example is the wine known in my neighborhood as "Wow!" By late May, one year, a batch of wine had finished fermenting and had cleared.

On June 3, my kids decided to honor me with a birthday party. They were the hosts. I was to relax and enjoy. The invitations went out to everyone in the neighborhood whose house could be seen by a person standing on our roof. The party had 100 percent attendance.

The wine I provided from my cellar, some fifteen vintages, from eight-year-old dandelion to four-year-old Chablis to new-born Wow!

By the end of the party, all the wine had been well sampled, but almost three gallons of Wow! were consumed. Even the beer chilled in tubs of ice didn't disappear as fast.

Yes, I am going to round off this introductory chapter by providing a couple of recipes for making relatively uncomplicated wine. If you're really serious about winemaking, there are dozens of books to read, but don't become discouraged until you try these two recipes I offer.

One important factor you will read about — and please believe it — is that the secret to winemaking is cleanliness. I keep a solution of winemaker's sodium metabisulfite available all the time, and all my equipment gets disinfected before I use it. If you "keep it clean," too, you'll enjoy making these wines.

WOW!

The wine known as "Wow!" in my neighborhood is not difficult to make. Neither is it difficult to drink. Many regular wine drinkers have learned to love it, and I have noticed a few non-wine drinkers sneaking back for seconds, yes, and even thirds.

You'll need these basic items — a 5-gallon carboy, a drilled cork and a bubbler. Plus the following ingredients:

9 pounds sugar, inverted
2 tablespoons lemon juice
concentrate
7 quarts bottled grape juice, with
no added ingredients (obtain
from any grocery store)
Water to fill carboy as directed
2-1/2 teaspoons yeast nutrient
1 bottle (1/2-ounce size) Vierke
Tokaier liquid yeast (a brand
imported from Germany; find
it in a winemakers' shop)

First, invert the sugar according to directions in the recipe for Family Table Wine, page 3.

Combine the grape juice and inverted sugar in the 5-gallon carboy. Fill with water to within 5 inches of top of carboy. Let stand overnight to reach room temperature and then add the yeast nutrient and the liquid yeast. Gently shake the bottle to stir.

Fermentation will usually not be evident for 2 days. Allow the mixture to work for 4 weeks and then check for alcohol percentage. Anywhere from 10 to 13 percent is usable. For some reason I can't explain, this wine ends its fermentation period nearly clear and finishes clearing in a short time if stored in a cool place. It can be bottled or served fresh. I made 5 batches before I could save enough to bottle. Wow!

McNUTT'S MULLED WINE

Years ago my family had a friend named McNutt, who was from Scotland by way of an adventurous life at sea. Oh, how he loved to tell us about his life! I can see him still, sitting in my folks' living room with glass in hand — but not filled with whiskey! His drink was mulled wine.

McNutt mulled his wine by heating it on the stove, but he never failed to tell us that it was supposed to be done by taking a red-hot poker from the fireplace and plunging it into a pitcher of wine. Can you hear the sizzle? But try McNutt's way and mine. It's safer.

1 fifth red wine
1 teaspoon honey
1/2 teaspoon lemon juice
1 stick cinnamon
2 whole cloves

Combine the wine and honey in a pan and stir over low heat. Add the lemon, cinnamon and cloves. Continue stirring until the liquid almost boils. Remove from the heat and serve in mugs. Think of the Scottish Highlands and enjoy.

WOOD-STACKERS' GLOGG

In the fall of '79, just before the first snow, we had a party at our house for our children and their muscles. It was time, you see, to stack three cords of wood against the upwind side of the house. On the downwind side, who could find three cords of wood in an eight-foot snowdrift? The Matanuska wind plays strange games with snow.

When the chore was finished, the crew retreated into the house for a hot drink. Some had chocolate, but most tried what I call Wood-Stackers' Glogg. The recipe is flexible. Ours goes like this:

2 quarts cranberry or cran-apple
juice
2 fifths red wine, of your own
making, perhaps
1-1/2 cups sugar

1-1/2 cups water (from a deep well
or spring, if possible)
2 2-inch sticks cinnamon
6 cardamom pods, crushed
8 whole cloves

We used a large, stainless steel mixing bowl for our Glogg, but any heat-proof bowl would do nicely. In the bowl, combine all the ingredients. Cover and chill 4 to 6 hours. This allows time for the proper blending of flavors.

When serving time comes, warm the Glogg in the container, bringing it to a comfortable drinking temperature. Serve it in cups with handles. For festive occasions, drop into each cup one or more orange slices, nuts, raisins or even a dried apricot. Surprise!

RECEPTION PUNCH

At the wedding reception for one of my daughters, we served a punch that was a howling success. I announced that the two bowls at the table contained the same punch, except that the one on the left was spiked with vodka; the right one wasn't.

Several days after the party my daughter described what happened to her that day. First I brought her a cup of left punch. Then so did both her grandfathers, one grandmother, and three of my trooper buddies.

In fact, I refilled the left punch bowl three times. The next morning I had almost a full bowl of punch left (right). *Right!*

This is the recipe we used:

1 gallon cranberry juice
1 12-ounce can frozen orange juice
    concentrate
1 6-ounce can frozen lemonade
    concentrate
2 quarts lime-lemon soda
1 quart water from a deep well
    or spring

Mix together in a large punch bowl and serve — right! It's even better, left: add such imaginative things as vodka, cold duck, or your own wine, in place of the soda. Left is all right. But right is not all left.

BROCCOLI CROWNED FISH

I first tried this recipe when I lived in Juneau a few years ago. I caught the fish and bought the broccoli. Yesterday I bought the fish and picked the broccoli out of my garden. The dish is good either way. Use any white-fleshed fish, such as sole, halibut, cod or haddock.

24 fresh broccoli flowerettes
4 white fish fillets,
*   about 8 ounces each*
Salt and pepper
2 tablespoons butter, melted
1/2 cup sour cream
1/2 cup mayonnaise
1 tablespoon finely minced onion
*   or scallion*
1 teaspoon horseradish
1/4 teaspoon dried dill weed or a
*   sprinkle of dill seed*
1 egg white

Steam broccoli in a basket over boiling water for 2 minutes. Remove basket from heat and set aside.

Salt and pepper fish to taste and brush with melted butter. Broil 5 minutes on one side and 3 minutes on the other.

While the fish is broiling mix together the sour cream, mayonnaise, onion, horseradish and dill in a medium-sized bowl. In a second bowl beat the egg white until it forms stiff peaks. Fold into the sour cream mixture.

Spread the steamed broccoli evenly on the fish fillets and cover with the egg and sour cream mixture.

Slide the fish under the broiler for 2 minutes or until the topping is golden brown. Serve at once. Delightful!

SQUIRRELING

CHAPTER 2

Each of the summers since my first book was published, I have kept the cover on the typewriter much of the time so that I could dedicate myself to my land, known as Blue Frog Farm. I planted a vast garden, did considerable landscaping, and sneaked off to go fishing once in a while.

The gardens have been great successes and have provided us with large quantities of food, both for summer experimenting and storing for winter.

Each fall found us with a full root cellar, a full Deepfreeze and ideas running out our ears about how to prepare the wealth of food.

In fact my daughter accuses me of being a squirrel, so vigorous are my efforts to store food. But I firmly deny hiding any nuts in the trees and fall back on my old excuse: I was a Depression child. Need I say more? Security is knowing there are 700 pounds of potatoes in the root cellar.

On the subject of potatoes, much to my surprise, I discovered a new way of preparing them last summer when we stopped for breakfast at a roadhouse in the high country. We were served ham, eggs, and . . . dirty potatoes.

At first glance I thought that they had been grated and cooked without benefit of *either* washing or peeling. I turned over some of the creepy things with my fork to find that I was partly wrong. The potatoes had been baked with their jackets on, then cooled and grated — still without peeling — and fried like hashbrowns.

Always a food gambler, I lifted a small helping with my fork and popped it into my mouth. The potatoes had been browned tenderly with some sautéed onions and were excellent. Since then I often bake a couple of extra potatoes at dinner time so we can have dirty potatoes for breakfast. I highly recommend that you try them.

The rest of that trip was enjoyable, too,

because we returned to parts of Alaska in which we once lived. But as a search for further food experiences, it was a bust. In one seaport town, we were served a meal of dry, tasteless fish that rivals the worst meal I have ever been asked to eat.

The worst meal was an old, long-dead tomcod forced on me by the hunger that can accumulate during a two-day wait for a delayed plane. At least the old tom wasn't tasteless.

Being stranded and hungry in the Bush is not an uncommon experience for those who travel about Alaska. Even with careful stocking, the grub box can come up empty before you run out of trip. The eternal optimist who thinks, "We can always live off the country!" is insane. Planning to eat moose, squirrel, fish or wombat is probably the surest way to have a gameless trip.

Back when I was discovering this form of insanity, I remember reaching an evening when only a single can of peas stood between bed without supper and three hungry men, until a crazy duck mistook our fire for a landing light. One lucky "B-a-loom!" from a shotgun changed the menu to duck stew.

Another problem in stocking the grub box wisely is that the man who eats like a bird in town invariably turns glutton in the Bush. Such a man accompanied me on a trip one fall, and he nearly starved the rest of our group. In town he was a secret daytime drinker, but we insisted on no alcohol until after dinner in the evening. To substitute for the constant stream of calories his drinking usually supplied, he raided the grub box when no one was looking. It was empty three days before we had planned to go home!

MATANUSKA FISH STEW

The world is blessed with many wonderful recipes for seafood soups and stews. In my mind, though, this one has no equal, not even the French bouillabaisse.

2 pounds white fish cut into
    1-inch cubes
2 tablespoons salad oil
1 cup chopped onion
2 cloves garlic, minced
1 chopped green pepper
1 No. 2½ can (1 lb. 13 oz.) tomatoes
3 chicken bouillon cubes
1/4 teaspoon thyme, crumbled
1/4 teaspoon basil, crumbled
1 cup white wine
1 cup water
1 7-1/2-ounce can minced clams
Salt and pepper

Add oil to a 5-quart Dutch oven. Over medium heat, sauté the onions, garlic and green pepper. Add the can of tomatoes, with juice, the bouillon cubes, thyme, basil, wine and water. Simmer on medium heat for 20 minutes, breaking up the tomatoes as you stir.

Add the cubes of fish and bring the liquid to a boil for 8 to 10 minutes. Add the can of clams with juice. Salt and pepper to taste. Serve in soup bowls and top with a large glob of Lively Vegetable Dip. (See page 18.) Yield: 4 servings.

An accidental loss of the grub box is not uncommon either. Such a disaster happened to my neighbor, river-running Robert, and his friend Tom, who'd planned their trip with visions of drifting down the Slana River and sneaking up on a bull moose around every bend.

They had been on the river only minutes when they tangled with a sweeper that half swamped their boat. The soaking loosened all the labels from their canned goods and made cooking akin to Russian roulette. It also eliminated all their flour, corn meal and bread, though a bacon slab and a bourbon bottle came through fine.

Later striking a large rock, the boat again filled with water, completing the destruction of all remaining food, except the unmarked cans and the slab of bacon. Oh, yes, and the bourbon.

After spending half a day patching the boat, they set out next morning on the journey downriver. Travel was fast and mooseless. About three in the afternoon, they shot over a falls with only a three-foot drop — just enough to turn the boat end over end until the bow stuck in the river bottom. The two men hung onto the boat and watched the floatable part of their gear disappear.

A mile down the river the men came ashore, salvaging the boat, two rifles and that slab of bacon. The bourbon disappeared.

They camped for the night and built a big fire to dry their clothes and grill bacon for their only meal that day. Next day they walked out to the road. End of trip.

The other day I stopped by Robert's place to swap a lie or two about river running, watch a football game and eat a seafood dinner.

The two of us share a love of gardening and especially recipes that combine fish with garden produce — either fresh or some we've squirreled away. Some of our favorite recipes are included in this chapter.

ZALMON CREAM BREAKFAST

When the first frost of last year was predicted, I still had a number of zucchini squash on the vine. I couldn't let these old friends freeze to death, so I invited them in for breakfast. Mine.

2 cups cooked salmon (or a 1-pound can of salmon)
1/4 cup mayonnaise
2 teaspoons lemon juice
1/4 teaspoon garlic or onion salt
1/4 teaspoon dill seed
1/4 teaspoon Worcestershire
1/8 teaspoon cayenne
1 cup finely chopped zucchini
2 teaspoons capers, drained
1 cup sour cream
Bread for toast

In a bowl break up the salmon, removing any bones and skin. Add mayonnaise, lemon juice, garlic salt, dill, Worcestershire and cayenne. Mix thoroughly and set aside.

In a second bowl combine the zucchini, capers and sour cream. Toast 8 slices of bread. Spread each piece with the salmon mixture from bowl one and then a topping from bowl two. Garnish and serve. You'll most likely need more toast, but it's best made on demand.

LIVELY VEGETABLE DIP

I love to wander through my garden and greenhouse and nibble on the many things that taste good. I can have a banquet in the backyard. Last year we added Sugar Snap peas to the garden. You can eat them pod and all, raw, blanched or cooked.

All of these good raw foods followed me into the house and there seemed to cry out for a good dip to enhance their flavor. This dip came to me as part of a fish recipe I'll include, too. It is excellent on both fresh vegetables and fish.

1-1/2 cups mayonnaise
2 cloves garlic, minced fine
1 teaspoon cayenne
2 tablespoons white vinegar
1/4 teaspoon salt

Combine all ingredients, mix well and chill for an hour or so before serving. Dip a flowerette of cauliflower, a thin slice of carrot, or a Sugar Snap pea into this and reach for another!

QUICK ZUCCHINI DELIGHT

Every summer, while I'm passing out the surplus zucchini, I hear the same question, "How do I cook it?"

This special recipe is my stock response:

3 tablespoons butter
1 large onion, sliced in thin
half-slices
1-1/2 cups zucchini squash, sliced
crosswise in 1/4-inch slices
1 15-ounce can stewed tomatoes
Salt and pepper
1/4 cup grated Parmesan cheese

In a heavy skillet with a cover, melt the butter and sauté the onions until they just turn transparent. Add the zucchini slices and saute for another 5 minutes. Add tomatoes and cook for another 5 minutes. Cover the skillet and reduce heat to low. Simmer for a final 10 minutes. Salt and pepper to taste.

Turn the vegetables into a serving dish, sprinkle with the Parmesan cheese and serve.

CARROT TOPPED HALIBUT

The carrots we grow in the Matanuska Valley are sweet and good, both raw and cooked. In my search for new ways to cook them, I acquired this recipe a couple of years ago and even bought some ramekins so I could try it. Any white-fleshed fish can be used.

2 pounds halibut, cut into 2-inch
*   pieces*
6 tablespoons butter, divided
2 cups shredded or grated carrots
2 tablespoons lemon juice
1/4 teaspoon finely grated
*   lemon peel*
1/4 teaspoon salt
1/4 teaspoon thyme
3 tablespoons flour
1/2 cup undiluted evaporated milk
*   or fresh cream*

Divide the fish pieces evenly between 4 ramekins. Melt 3 tablespoons of butter and brush it on the fish. Mix carrots, lemon juice, peel, salt and thyme together and divide the mixture evenly over the fish. Cover the ramekins tightly and bake at 450° for 35 minutes, or until the fish is done.

Remove the ramekins and hold the fish carefully as you drain the liquid into a bowl. Save the liquid. Keep the fish warm as you do the next step.

In a saucepan, over medium heat, combine the remaining 3 tablespoons of butter and the flour to create a roux. Remove from the heat and add 1-1/2 cups of fish liquid and the milk or cream. Return to heat and stir until thickened. Salt and pepper to taste and pour over the fish. Serve at once in the ramekins.

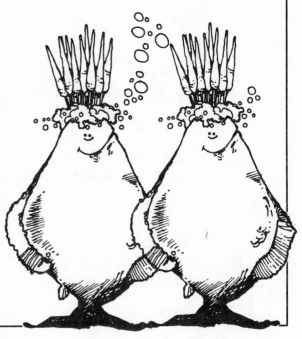

CHARD BAKED FISH

The garden in back of the house produces another favorite — Swiss chard. Cooked with thinly sliced onions and tiny slivers of bacon, it's wonderful. Only I could make it fattening. I like it cooked any way, even stuffed in a fish.

1 whole, dressed fish, 3 to 5 pounds
    (red snapper, sea bass,
    rockfish)
1-1/2 teaspoons salt, divided
1/2 cup chopped onion
1-1/2 cups chopped celery
1/2 cup butter or margarine,
    divided
4 cups 1/4-inch bread cubes
4 cups Swiss chard (or spinach),
    washed and drained
1 teaspoon lemon juice
1/4 teaspoon pepper

The fish must be fresh or fully thawed. Rinse well in water and dry. Sprinkle half the salt inside and outside the fish.

Sauté the onions and celery in 6 tablespoons of butter until tender. Add bread cubes and chard and cook over medium heat until chard is tender. Add the remaining salt, lemon juice and pepper and toss. Stuff the cavity of the fish, closing the edges with lacing or skewers. Brush the fish with the remaining butter.

Bake at 350° for 60 minutes. The fish is done when it flakes easily. Serve with baked potatoes and cook a couple extra. For breakfast, remember?

You don't remember?

Well, at the beginning of this chapter I told you about some "dirty potatoes" Connie and I ate for breakfast one morning at a roadhouse in the high country. But looks are deceiving. Dirty potatoes are well worth planning in advance for breakfast some morning. You need cold, prebaked potatoes which you then grate — leave the jackets on! — and prepare like hashbrowns. See page 13 for the full description.

HIGH MOUNTAIN IRISH STEW

I have in my files no less than eight "authentic" recipes for Irish stew. Some state that the meat in this stew originally was kid, while others mention lamb. A camp cook gave me the following recipe after a whole camp full of sheep hunters raved over the stew he produced one rainy afternoon. I would highly recommend that you try using mountain sheep meat if you have it available. Or use lamb, kid, or even veal or beef, and you will still have "authentic" Irish stew.

3 pounds stew meat — mountain sheep, lamb, kid, or beef, cut into 1-inch cubes
1/2 cup flour
3 tablespoons vegetable oil
12 medium potatoes, peeled; 2 of them thinly sliced; the rest whole
1 cup sliced carrots
4 cups sliced onion
2 cloves garlic, minced
1/2 pound slab bacon, cut into 1-inch cubes
1 No. 2½ can (1 lb. 13 oz.) tomatoes
2 teaspoons salt
1 teaspoon thyme, crumbled
1/4 teaspoon black pepper
2 cups beef stock

Shake the meat pieces and flour in a paper sack. Add the oil to your Dutch oven over medium heat. Brown the meat, a few pieces at a time, and remove to a bowl. Scrape as much residue as you can out of the pan along with the meat.

Put a layer of sliced potatoes in the bottom of the Dutch oven and cover it with a layer of carrots. Now add a layer of onions and a sprinkle of garlic. Next return the browned meat to the pan and add bacon cubes. Dump in the tomatoes and spread them around. Add remaining carrots and onions, followed by the salt, thyme, pepper and beef stock. Last, place whole potatoes on top of the other ingredients.

Cover the Dutch oven tightly and slide the pan into a 350° oven for 2-1/2 hours. Or simmer on a stove or campfire.

Like any other stew, this one is best served in deep bowls with huge chunks of good bread or biscuits.

McSHEA THEORY OF COOKING

CHAPTER
3

According to historian Randolf Z. McShea, the art of cooking could have developed right here in Alaska. We are aware that this land once grew mastodon because we still wash their carcasses out of the permafrost every year or so. As man began his life on earth in the era of the mastodon, he must have been here in Alaska. So McShea theorizes.

Taking his theory for fact, let's imagine our soon-to-be-famous caveman, Smog. He isn't as pretty as you and I, but he is remarkably equipped to survive in his environment. For the sake of the story, let's say he has already discovered fire. He is about to discover cooking.

On the eventful day, Smog finds an egg about the size of a football. He tucks it under his arm and makes a run for the goal — I mean cave. As he passes a hot

spring he fumbles and drops the ball into the pool of hot water. Alas, it lies there in the white sand wiggling slightly in the current.

Smog picks up a forked stick — maybe the very one that later becomes the first barbecue fork — and with another stick as prop fishes the egg out of the pool. Seven long minutes are used to fish out the egg. . . . All right, three minutes if you like eggs soft-boiled. As soon as it is cool enough to carry, Smog is off for home. Little does he know he is making the first fast-food delivery.

Smog's wife Tingle is truly surprised to find the interior of the egg solid. The taste meets with her approval, and she soon has Smog dropping eggs in the pool regularly. But after a time, as I imagine the story, Smog takes Tingle by the hand — or hair,

BEER-DRINKERS' STEW

This is a peppy but not over-powering stew that requires plenty of accompanying cold beer. The friend who first served it to me also made the beer we drank. On the morning of the third day I spent at his house, he sobered up long enough to scratch the stew recipe on a paper sack, just before I caught a plane home. He didn't name it, so I did my best.

3 pounds stew meat (beef, moose or what-have-you), cut into 1-inch cubes
1 tablespoon cider vinegar
1 tablespoon lime juice (lemon okay, too)
1 tablespoon chili powder
1 12-ounce can V-8 juice
2 tablespoons salad oil
2 cups thinly sliced onion
1 4-ounce can green chilies
2 cloves garlic, minced fine
1 tablespoon fresh ginger, minced
1/4 teaspoon ground turmeric
1-1/2 teaspoons salt
1 15-ounce can tomatoes

Combine vinegar, lime juice, chili powder and V-8 juice in a bowl. Add meat and marinate for 20 minutes. Stir occasionally.

Heat oil in a large frying pan or Dutch oven and sauté the onions, chilies and garlic over low heat. When the onions are translucent, add ginger, turmeric and salt. Mix well and add tomatoes, breaking them with a spoon. Next add the meat and marinade to the pan and simmer, stirring often, for 1-1/2 hours. Add water if more liquid is necessary. When the meat is tender, the stew is done.

Serve it straight from the pan to deep bowls, accompanied by hard rolls and beer. Or pour stew into a ring of rice molded in a deep dish. Serves 6. With beer!

more likely — and escorts her to the pool, where one or two swift slaps completes the world's first course in cooking.

Smog doesn't get out of the cooking task so easily, however, for now Tingle insists that he escort her to the hot spring to protect her from saber-toothed tigers. Soon Smog sculpts a pot out of a soft rock near the cave.

That rock, filled with water and set beside the fire, was the start of the modern kitchen. Man was now boiling his food.

Imagine the fun Tingle and Smog had with their discovery. They learned that many things tasted better boiled. Granted, birds tasted better if the feathers were removed first.

One day Tingle had a fat chunk of meat boiling in her stone pot. The family left the cave to engage in a small war or maybe to confront the old saber-toothed tiger again. They returned to find the pot boiled dry and the meat sizzling away in its own fat. It smelled and tasted different — and good. Frying had been born.

Several days later Tingle left a piece of meat frying in the stone. It smelled heavenly to their almost tame pet wolf, and he stole it for himself. Thereafter Smog and Tingle placed a large flat rock over the frying meat, creating the first covered roaster.

Though progress was especially rapid in those days, new ideas for cooking continue to be invented nearly every time you turn around. Still, many times I feel close to Smog and Tingle, not just when I kneel beside a campfire and shove a Dutch oven into the coals, but even lifting a pan onto the electric stove. I take a quick glance over my shoulder for the saber-toothed tiger or the Alaska brown bear or to count how many extras the kids have brought home for dinner. It's all the same.

Despite the enormous difference between my kitchen and theirs, my favorite eating is often — just as theirs

KNIK GOULASH HUNGARIAN

In years past, the people who lived along the Knik River in the Matanuska Valley expected an annual flood. A glacier pressed against a mountain and formed a dam each winter. Then along about the middle of each summer, the dam broke. I was sixteen and visiting a family who lived in the flood plain when the dam broke one year. Suddenly we were isolated on a very small island, about 100 feet around.

The flood was incidental; more important is that the woman of the house served something she called "real Hungarian goulash." I suspect now that she let the contents drift a bit from the original recipe, but there were some extra mouths to feed that night. For instance I never again found potatoes in a recipe for Hungarian goulash. Whatever its authenticity, it is worth trying.

3 pounds stew meat, beef or moose,
*   cut into 1-inch cubes*
4 slices bacon
Salad oil
2 cups chopped onion
1 or 2 cloves garlic
1/4 teaspoon cayenne
1/4 teaspoon caraway seed
1 tablespoon paprika
1 12-ounce can beer, opened and
*   gone flat*
1 cup beef stock
1 No. 2½ can (1 lb. 13 oz.) tomatoes
4 cups potatoes, well washed and
*   cut into 1-inch dice*

1-1/2 teaspoons salt
1 16-ounce can cut green beans
1/3 cup flour

In your Dutch oven, cook the bacon until it is crisp. Leave the grease and remove the bacon. Dredge the meat in flour and brown a few pieces at a time and remove to a bowl. If the bacon drippings are skimpy, add a little salad oil during browning. Remove the last of the browned meat from the pan.

Add enough salad oil to the pan to sauté the onions and garlic until tender. Stir in the cayenne, caraway seed and paprika and return the beef to the pan.

Add beer, beef stock and cooked bacon and bring to a simmer for 90 minutes.

Add the tomatoes, with their liquid, the salt and potatoes. Continue simmering for 30 minutes. Then add the green beans.

Combine remaining flour with a little stew liquid or water and stir it into the stew. Bring to a boil until the liquid thickens.

Serve in deep bowls so that every drop of gravy can be eaten. It will serve 6. Enjoy!

must have been — the one-pot meal, or good, old-fashioned stew.

My friend Ted-the-Stew-Lover maintains that you can start with a basic Smog-and-Tingle meat and vegetable stew and, with the judicious choice of spices we've discovered since their time, create a flavor to match the taste expectations of almost any ethnic group.

For an Oriental stew you add a touch of soy sauce and a hint of ginger. You could also add bamboo shoots, water chestnuts, mushrooms and bean sprouts. Adding caraway seed, paprika, and perhaps some sauerkraut, will produce a near-authentic Hungarian goulash. For the Flemish taste, add thyme and nutmeg. For Mexican, add cumin, oregano, cayenne, green chilies and so on.

Though Ted's theory that spice is the variety of stew has plenty of merit and nearly endless possibilities, I believe the kind of meat is as important.

The meat in my mother's stew pot was not always beef or chicken but venison, caribou, moose, ptarmigan, grouse, squirrel, marmot and, yes, even porcupine. In other words, the meat *du jour* was what we could catch and it established the variety of stew. On the days when nothing was caught, Mother fixed an old standby — bacon stew. When the bacon was gone, we had vegetable stew. That's about as far down the scale as I can remember her ever going.

I have found a number of interesting recipes from my files that will stir you to stew making. Think of Smog and Tingle — and Ted and Mother — when you start adding things to the pot. Good eating!

SOUTHEASTERN CHICKEN STEW

I first tasted this stew in a restaurant in Ketchikan. I liked it so much I tried to ask the chef for his recipe. He wouldn't talk to me.

Upset by this seeming inhospitality, I complained to a local friend about it. Only then did I discover that the chef wouldn't talk to me because he couldn't. He did not speak English. Some months later, my friend sent this recipe with a Christmas card. I am pleased to be able to share the chef's hospitality with you.

12 chicken thighs
3 tablespoons vegetable oil
2 cups halved and sliced onion
1 15-ounce can tomatoes
1/4 cup chili sauce or ketchup
1 teaspoon salt
1/4 teaspoon pepper
1/2 cup dried apricots
1/2 cup dried, pitted prunes
1 green pepper, chopped
2 10-ounce packages frozen okra

Place your Dutch oven on medium heat and add the oil. Brown chicken pieces, 3 at a time, and set aside. Add onion to the oil and sauté until tender. Return chicken to the pan.

Add tomatoes with their liquid and break into pieces. Add chili sauce, salt and pepper. Cover and simmer over low heat for 50 minutes.

Add apricots, prunes, green pepper and stir well. Cook, covered, for 5 minutes. Add the okra, return cover and cook for an additional 10 minutes. Be sure the okra is under the liquid during cooking. It should be tender but still slightly crisp.

Yield: 4 to 6 servings.

GRETTA'S GERMAN STEW

Gretta was a war bride following World War II. She had a ready smile, a big heart, and was brave enough to marry a GI in Germany and go home with him to Alaska. She was also a good cook.

After her husband and I hunted together one fall we were all overstocked with moose ribs. They invited Connie and me over for what Gretta called "Fefferpothast." (My spelling, of course.) Now you know why I renamed it.

4 pounds short ribs, moose or beef, cut into about 2-inch-wide sections
1/4 cup vegetable oil
1 teaspoon salt
1 teaspoon black pepper, freshly ground
6 large onions, sliced
1 quart beef stock
1/8 teaspoon cayenne
8 whole cloves
4 bay leaves
1 lemon
1 tablespoon capers
1-1/2 cups pumpernickel bread crumbs

Drag out the Dutch oven one more time, put it on medium heat, and add the vegetable oil. Salt and pepper the rib pieces and brown them a few at a time. Remove to a bowl as they are browned.

Sauté the onions in the oil and meat residue until they are tender. Return meat to the pot and add beef stock and cayenne. The cloves and bay leaves should be tied in a cheesecloth bag (for easy removal later) and then dropped into the pot. Bring liquid to a boil and simmer stew for 2 hours.

Carefully remove the meat and onions from the pot and set aside in a warming dish. Remove and discard the cheesecloth bag. You may wish to bone the meat at this time, but it isn't necessary.

Skim most of the fat off the liquid in the pot to prepare it for sauce. Carefully peel the outer rind from the lemon. Slice the peel in thick strips and add to the pot. Then squeeze the juice from the pulp into the pot. Bring the liquid back to a boil and add capers. Stir in the bread crumbs and simmer, uncovered, for 15 minutes.

The final step is to fish the lemon peel from the sauce, arrange the meat on a platter and pour the sauce over it. Serve with boiled potatoes or rice.

Now I remember how Gretta translated the German name. She called it "Pepperpot." By any name it is excellent. Pass the beer.

FLEMISH STEW SKILAK

I still remember my last hunting trip in the company of my father-in-law when we camped near Skilak Lake on the Kenai Peninsula. Not for him were cold tents and kneeling beside a campfire to cook. The only "roughing it" of the trip occurred when he turned the thermostat in his motorhome down to 65° at night. A sure sign of maturity on my part, I loved it.

After the first day's hunting, Crocket demonstrated the extent of his faith in our ability to "live off the land." He reached into the refrigerator and brought out the makings for the following stew.

2-1/2 pounds beef stew meat, cut
into 1-inch cubes
1/2 cup flour
3 tablespoons vegetable oil
1-1/2 cups chopped onion
1/4 teaspoon garlic salt
1 teaspoon thyme, crushed
1/4 teaspoon ground nutmeg
1-1/2 teaspoons salt
1/4 teaspoon pepper
1/2 teaspoon parsley flakes
1 12-ounce can flat beer
13 pitted, dried prunes

With the burner set on medium, Crocket placed a Dutch oven on the stove and added the oil. He shook cubes of meat in a paper bag with the flour and then browned them. He added the onions, garlic salt, thyme, nutmeg, and stirred to coat everything well. Then the salt, pepper, parsley, beer and prunes went into the pot. He brought the contents to a boil, covered the pot and let it simmer for 90 minutes.

While the stew was cooking, Crocket slipped a few hard sourdough buns into the oven to toast. These he split, buttered and cubed in 1-inch chunks. When serving time came, he threw a handful of these bread chunks into each bowl and covered them with stew. They were the best bread cubes I ever tasted. Oh, yes. The stew was fantastic, too.

NO BREAD COMBINATION GOULASH (and dumplings)

During February of 1979, the Matanuska wind tried its best to blow our house away. For ten solid days it shook and rattled and tried to roll us up the hill. Our driveway and access road were buried under six- to eight-foot snowdrifts, and we were snowbound, as were hundreds of others during that storm.

By the eighth day we were out of bread and nearly out of flour. Just a scant two cups remained in the bin. I found myself staring into the Deep-freeze out in the garage. Three frozen pork chops and a pound of stew meat stared back. My mind said, "Goulash!"

If you are an avid goulash fan, bear with me in this emergency effort, which turned out pretty darn good.

1 pound beef or moose, cut in
  stew chunks
1 pound pork, cut in stew chunks
3 tablespoons salad oil
2 cups chopped onion
1 or 2 cloves garlic
1 cup thinly sliced carrots
1/2 teaspoon caraway seed
2 cups beef stock (or 4 bouillon
  cubes and 2 cups water)
1 teaspoon paprika
1 8-ounce can sauerkraut

Into your trusty Dutch oven pour the oil. Brown the meat, both beef and pork, over medium heat. Remove meat and set aside.

In the same pan sauté the onions, garlic and carrots until onions are transparent. Return meat to the pan and add caraway seed, beef stock and paprika. Cover and simmer for 1 hour.

Next add the sauerkraut and taste, adding salt, if desired. Return cover and simmer another 10 minutes until kraut is thoroughly heated.

You could serve this dish with bread, but we didn't have any bread on that first occasion. Instead we added dumplings to the top of the goulash. To make dumplings, you can grab the box of biscuit mix, or do what we did:

Combination Goulash Dumplings
1 egg
2/3 cup milk
1/2 teaspoon salt
1 tablespoon baking powder
1-1/2 cups all-purpose flour

Whip egg and milk together. Fold in salt, baking powder and flour. Stir until the mixture is damp. Gently place by spoonfuls — about 8 of them — on top of hot goulash. Return cover and simmer for about 20 minutes.

MATANUSKA RAGOUT OF VEAL

Shortly after moving back to the Matanuska Valley to retire, I became acquainted with Tom while shopping in a supermarket. As one of many subjects, we discussed the difficulty of finding good veal, and he raved about a favorite specialty of his, ragout of veal. I buttered him up and became downright pushy for the recipe, but he topped all my expectations by inviting me to dinner. This is what he served.

4 pounds boneless veal shoulder,
    cut into 1-1/4-inch cubes
Water to cover
7 cups chicken stock (or 9 chicken
    bouillon cubes and 7 cups
    water)
2 cups sliced carrots
1 onion, studded with 3 whole
    cloves
1 teaspoon thyme, crumbled
1 teaspoon salt
1 bay leaf
1/2 cup butter, divided
2 cups small, whole onions
1/2 pound small, whole
    mushrooms
3 tablespoons flour
2 egg yolks
White pepper and parsley
1 cup heavy cream
1 teaspoon lemon juice

The Dutch oven is going to be used again. First place the meat in the pan and cover with water. Bring to a boil for a minute or two. Skim off any scum. Then drain the meat into a colander.

Rinse the pot and return the meat to it along with 6 cups of the chicken stock. Add carrots, clove-studded onion, thyme, salt and bay leaf. Return to a boil, skim again and simmer, partly covered, for 1 hour.

In a second pan add the remaining 1 cup chicken stock and 3 tablespoons of the butter. Cook the small onions until they are tender. With a slotted spoon, carefully remove them to a large bowl and set aside. To the same pan and liquid, add the mushrooms. Cook for 10 minutes and remove to the bowl with the onions. Retain the liquid.

When the meat is tender, remove it to the bowl with the onions. Next, line a strainer with cheesecloth. Strain the onion-mushroom liquid and the meat-cooking liquid. Retain the resulting stock.

In a saucepan, melt the remaining 3 tablespoons of butter. Stir in the flour and make a roux. Cook for 2 minutes over medium heat. Be careful not to brown the roux. Add 3 cups of the vegetable-meat stock and turn the heat to high. Stir constantly until mixture starts to thicken. Reduce the heat to low and cook for 10 minutes. Remove from the heat.

Beat the egg yolks and cream together and slowly stir this mixture into the thickened stock to create a sauce. Add lemon juice and white pepper to taste. Now wash and dry the Dutch oven. Drain the meat and vegetables of all juices that have accumulated under them and spoon the solids back into the Dutch oven. Pour the sauce over them and stir over medium heat until the meat is hot again. Please DO NOT allow the contents to come to a boil.

Serve the ragout in deep dishes, garnished with parsley, if in season. Believe me, it is well worth the effort to make.

HUNTER'S PORK STEW

Since I was raised in Alaska, I didn't even see a pig until I was over sixteen, let alone hunt one. This recipe must have found its way to my files from the days when my great-grandparents had a farm. I've added a few ingredients and like the results.

3 pounds country-style pork ribs,
*   cut to serving size*
1-1/2 teaspoons salt, divided
1/4 teaspoon pepper, divided
6 large onions, quartered
2 apples, quartered and cored
1 teaspoon brown sugar
6 medium potatoes, whole,
*   unpeeled*
1-1/2 cups water
1 tablespoon Worcestershire

Into your Dutch oven place salted and peppered pieces of pork rib. Spread them across the bottom and add a layer of onions and remaining salt and pepper. Add apples and sprinkle with brown sugar. Now add the potatoes and 1-1/2 cups water. Last, add the Worcestershire sauce. Bring to a boil, cover and simmer for 2-1/2 hours. The stew is done when the ribs are tender.

I usually place the Dutch oven in the middle of the dining table and deal the soup bowls. Warm, buttered French bread completes this meal with style. Four of us enjoyed it the last time I made it.

SPAGHETTI BROCCOLI

Each year, more of my garden space is planted in broccoli. We eat it fresh, raw or steamed, and freeze up to a hundred packages every year. We even find ourselves giving some away late in the season. A neighbor who received some of our broccoli brought me this recipe, or one *almost* like it. I can't resist adding to a recipe I like.

1 pound spaghetti, cooked as
    package directs
6 tablespoons butter, divided
2 cups fresh cherry tomatoes
1 clove garlic, minced
1/2 teaspoon salt
1 teaspoon sweet basil leaves,
    crumbled
1 cup chicken stock (or 2 bouillon
    cubes and 1 cup water)
6 cups fresh broccoli cut into 1-inch
    pieces
1/2 cup Parmesan cheese
1/2 cup Brazil nuts, slivered
Fresh parsley, for garnish (optional)

In a Dutch oven, melt 2 tablespoons of the butter over medium heat. Add tomatoes and cook 5 minutes, stirring often. They should be tender but still hold their shape. Add garlic, salt and sweet basil and cook for another 2 minutes. Remove to a side dish and keep warm.

Add chicken stock to the empty Dutch oven, followed by the broccoli. Bring to a boil and simmer for 5 minutes. Broccoli should be tender but still firm; adjust cooking time accordingly. Remove broccoli from pan and keep warm. Drain and reserve the cooking liquid.

Melt 2 more tablespoons of butter in the pan and add the cooked and drained spaghetti. Toss until it is well coated with butter. Add tomatoes, broccoli, a half-cup of the reserved liquid and the cheese. Toss again to blend. Add more liquid if needed.

Dish the spaghetti into a serving bowl and garnish with nuts and parsley. I usually make additional cheese available. The spaghetti will stand on its own, but a good dry wine and garlic bread makes the meal a feast. Yield: 4 servings.

ALASKA PASTA

CHAPTER 4

During my twenty-one years as an Alaska State Trooper, I traveled much of the state, sometimes visiting places few people ever go. All too many of my trips were caused by other people wanting to get away from it all. When people go remote, the law often has to follow.

On one such trip I had to charter a plane to fly into a remote spot. My pilot pointed out the corrugated iron roof of the cabin I'd come to find and said, "That's old Tom's place. I'll drop you off at the lake about a mile ahead. There is a good trail."

I stood a moment on the shore of the lake and watched my link with civilization vanish into the sky before I turned, briefcase in hand, and began to walk.

I wasn't out there to drag old Tom off to jail, I should tell you. He is a God-fearing and honest old man. But he had been in an Anchorage bar when another man was shot, and the district attorney wanted to know if Tom's testimony was worth bringing him back as a witness at the trial.

The trail was good with a nice neat bridge over Fish Creek, which the pilot had also pointed out to me saying, "That's Fish Creek number 5,621." I certainly believed him. I have personally stepped or fallen into at least 341 of the Fish Creeks in Alaska.

As I walked the last hundred feet to the cabin, I was in the deep shadows of some trees. Looking ahead, I saw that the cabin's front porch roof cast a deep shadow there, too. In it was the dim figure of a man carrying a .30-30 rifle. When I stepped out of the shadow, old Tom saw my trooper's hat for the first time. He stepped off the porch, shifted the rifle to his left hand and shoved out his right hand to be shaken.

His grip was powerful enough that I was glad when he let go. "What brings you so far, Trooper?" he asked.

"You!" I said and quickly added, "I need a statement about what you saw in the Starlight Bar last April."

"Yep! I was there all right. I heard the shots but didn't see a damned thing! When is your plane coming back?"

I told him it would be back before dark. We went inside to handle the details of the written statement the D.A. required. Then, while I sat back drinking coffee, he set a Dutch oven on the stove and started cutting meat to go into it. "Ah! stew," I thought at first but discovered he was cutting the meat too fine for that. When the meat browned, filling the cabin with delightful smells, he started adding other things to the pot. "Spaghetti? Sloppy Joe sauce?" I wondered. It was beginning to make my mouth water.

The second big pot of water and the handful of spaghetti removed any doubt. I found myself hoping the pilot would be late. He was, and I didn't need an invitation to dinner. Old Tom just dished me up a large plateful when the spaghetti was done. To this he added a tin boxful of biscuits to sop up the extra sauce. More coffee finished the meal.

We had spaghetti again for breakfast. (For the two-hundredth time, a plane did not return for me when the pilot said it would.) Only then did Tom mention that the meat in the spaghetti was beaver. To this day, I think it was actually porcupine, but who argues with the host? And, no, I didn't get his recipe for the sauce! But some equally good ones are in this chapter.

STORMBOUND MACARONI

One miserable day in Southeastern, rough seas just outside our "hole-in-the-wall" harbor kept four of us huddled in the cabin of a small ship. Here's what our skipper served for the evening meal:

4 quarts boiling water
1 teaspoon salt
1 pound elbow macaroni (or the
     pasta you have)
1/2 cup vegetable oil (or bacon
     grease)
2 tablespoons butter (or margarine)
2 cloves garlic, minced (or
     1/2 teaspoon garlic powder)
2 7-1/2-ounce cans chopped clams
1-1/2 teaspoons oregano, crumbled
1/4 teaspoon pepper
1 tablespoon fresh snipped parsley
     (or 2 teaspoons dried parsley
     flakes)

Add salt and macaroni to boiling water and cook about 12 minutes. Drain and place in a serving dish.

While the pasta cooks, heat oil and butter in a skillet over medium heat and sauté the garlic. Add juice from the canned clams, oregano and pepper and simmer 10 minutes. Add clams and simmer another minute. Pour over macaroni and toss. Sprinkle on fresh parsley and toss again. Serves 4 nicely.

Note: If you use dried parsley, add it to the sauce with the oregano.

HEALTHY MACARONI

Though I am not a health food pusher, I don't mind assuring you there is absolutely nothing in this recipe that will *hurt* you. It's good eating, quick to prepare and Italian-sounding . . . health food enough for me! Try it.

4 quarts water
1/2 teaspoon salt
8 ounces whole-wheat elbow
     macaroni
2 tablespoons vegetable oil (olive oil
     preferred)
1 cup chopped onions
2 cloves garlic, minced
1 35-ounce can Italian-style
     tomatoes
1 teaspoon oregano, crumbled
1 teaspoon thyme, crumbled
Salt and pepper

In a large pot, bring water to a boil over high heat. Add salt and macaroni and cook as the package directs. (Timing may be different for whole-wheat pasta.)

Heat oil in a skillet over medium heat and sauté onions and garlic about 3 minutes. Add tomatoes, breaking them into pieces with a spoon. Stir in oregano, thyme and salt and pepper to taste. Bring to a boil, lower heat and simmer for 15 minutes.

To serve, place well-drained macaroni in a serving dish and pour the sauce over it. Accompany with a bowl of grated Parmesan, if desired.

NELSONI MEAT SAUCE

Almost all cooking generates memories of my first eating experiences. About pasta, however, my memory doesn't go too far back. For some unknown reason the women in our family were not great pasta fans, and they did most of the cooking.

At last, the Irish, English, Danish and French mixture of potato eaters in the family line has produced a pasta freak. I love the stuff and have been collecting recipes for many years. From the hundreds, I have selected a few favorites. Many of them start with my own special meat sauce.

My recipe may cause a few Italians to throw up their hands in disgust or frustration. But I dare even the fussiest pasta connoisseur to try the recipe and not like it!

3 pounds lean ground beef, moose
    or caribou
3 tablespoons vegetable oil
1/4 cup butter
3 cups chopped onion
4 cloves garlic, minced fine

1 cup finely chopped celery
1 teaspoon salt
1/2 teaspoon pepper
1 tablespoon sweet basil leaves,
    crumbled
1 tablespoon oregano leaves,
    crumbled
1 tablespoon dried parsley flakes
2 tablespoons chili powder
1 cup grated carrots
4 cups beef stock (or 6 bouillon
    cubes and 4 cups water)
2 6-ounce cans tomato paste
2 8-ounce cans tomato sauce
1 cup dry red wine
2 4-ounce cans mushroom stems
    and pieces

This recipe is going to make a lot of meat sauce. Start with a 6-quart pot or Dutch oven. Add the oil and half the meat. Brown it, breaking it into small pieces as it cooks over medium heat. Lift the first half out to a bowl and brown the second half. Remove this to the same bowl.

Wipe out the pot and return it to medium heat. Add butter, onions, garlic, and celery and sauté until the onions are transparent.

Combine salt, pepper, basil, oregano, parsley and chili powder in a bowl. Stir well and add to the onion mixture. Stir to coat everything with spices.

Add the carrots, stock, tomato paste, tomato sauce and wine. Stir well and return the meat to the pan. Bring to a boil and simmer for 1 hour. Add the mushrooms and set on low heat for another 15 minutes before serving.

The sauce can be served over spaghetti at once or used in a number of other pasta dishes. We often spoon it hot over buns or toast and make Sloppy Joes. Since it freezes very well, I always try to have leftover sauce for another meal. It's such a pleasant surprise to find it in the freezer later.

Remember, too, this sauce is better the second day, when the flavors have fully blended. I often make it the day before we are planning a spaghetti feed. That way I get the chance to spread some cold on a slice of bread and make a Nelsoni Meat Sauce sandwich. There are many ways to enjoy!

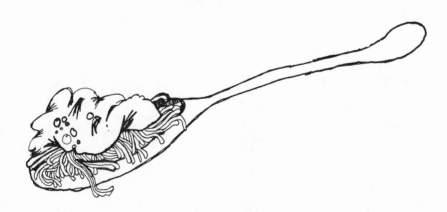

NELSONI
CORNMEAL BAKE

This recipe is in the chapter on pasta because cornmeal mush is good with Nelsoni Meat Sauce.

My mother trained me early in life to love cornmeal mush. We ate it hot with milk and sugar or honey. We had it chilled, sliced and fried, and served with lots of good butter and syrup in the morning for breakfast. When I was older, I discovered how good it is baked in a casserole with meat sauce.

To make cornmeal mush you'll need a heavy 3-quart saucepan, to which you add 3 cups water and 1 teaspoon salt. Bring it to a rapid boil over high heat. In a small bowl combine 1 cup corn meal and 1 cup cold water. Now pour the cornmeal mixture into the boiling water. Stir constantly until the mixture begins to thicken. Then reduce the heat, cover and cook for about 15 minutes. Lift the lid and stir twice during this cooking period.

Next you pour the hot cornmeal mush into a buttered 13 x 9 x 2-inch baking pan. Pop the pan into the refrigerator to cool and firm. Or out on the wood pile if the weather is cold enough. When the mush is firm, you are ready to proceed with Nelsoni Cornmeal Bake.

4 slices cold cornmeal mush, each about 3-1/2 x 3-1/2 inches
3 cups Nelsoni Meat Sauce
1-1/2 cups grated mozzarella cheese

Begin by laying the 4 slices of cornmeal mush in a buttered 8 x 8-inch square baking pan. Spoon half the sauce over and around the cornmeal pieces. Sprinkle half the cheese over the sauce. Add the remaining sauce and spread evenly. Add the final layer of cheese on top.

Bake at 350° for 30 minutes. Remove and let stand 10 minutes before serving. Yield: 4 servings. (On the other hand, if there are to be four people at the table, you should have doubled the recipe. Leftovers make wonderful midnight snacks.)

GREEN BEANS NELSONI

I know you're gasping, "Green beans in the pasta section?" Let me explain. This recipe was developed in an effort to "sell" a case of disliked French-cut green beans to my family. As anything tastes good under Nelsoni Meat Sauce, this dish resulted.

1 16-ounce can green beans,
*   French cut, or otherwise*
1/2 cup Nelsoni Meat Sauce
2 ounces grated mozzarella cheese

Heat the sauce in a pan over medium heat. Drain the green beans thoroughly and add to the sauce. When hot, sprinkle on the cheese and cover for 5 minutes. When the cheese is melted, serve. Yield: 4 vegetable servings.

CARROTED NOODLES

Did I mention that the Matanuska Valley grows the world's best carrots? Raw or simply cooked in butter they are tender little jewels. I also like them fixed this way:

24 ounces egg noodles, medium
*   or wide*
3/4 cup butter
6 cups shredded carrots
1-1/2 teaspoons salt
1-1/2 cups whole milk
1/4 teaspoon pepper
3/4 tablespoon parsley flakes
4 eggs, lightly beaten

Add noodles to boiling water in a large pan. Cook 4 minutes only. Drain in a colander. Melt the butter in the warm pan and return the noodles to it. Toss to coat evenly.

In a second pan cover the carrots with water and add the salt. Boil for 2 minutes. Drain in the colander and add to the noodles. Toss mixture again.

Combine milk, pepper, parsley and eggs in a bowl. Mix well and stir into the noodles and carrots.

Pour the mixture into a well-greased, 6-quart casserole. Cover and slide the casserole into a 375° oven for 45 minutes. Every 15 minutes, stir the mixture.

Serve the casserole with corn bread if possible. It will serve 4 to 6. Leftovers are good.

MAUDE'S
SAUSAGE SUPPER

The wife of one of my hunting partners always claimed she could put dinner for two weary and unsuccessful hunters on the table in 30 minutes. Late one moose season, her husband and I returned from a trip — in darkness — at 2:30 in the afternoon. We'd found 20-below weather, some down the back of the neck, but no moose. We came home hungry, and Maude, bless her heart, made good on her claim with this dish:

3/4 cup macaroni
1 medium onion, chopped
1/2 cup chopped green pepper
1 teaspoon salt
1 tablespoon Worcestershire
1-1/2 cups spaghetti sauce, canned or prepared Nelsoni Meat Sauce
1 pound smoked, Polish- or Italian-style sausage, cut into 1/4-inch slices.

Cook macaroni in 2 quarts of boiling water for 8 minutes.

While the macaroni is cooking, combine onions, green pepper, salt, Worcestershire, spaghetti sauce, and sausage in a heavy skillet or frying pan. Heat to simmer, stirring frequently.

When the macaroni is done, drain it in a colander and add to the skillet.

Stir well and cook for another 10 minutes, covered.

The recipe serves 2 amply and maybe more. Maude served it with sourdough French bread and lots of Parmesan cheese.

SPAGHETTI la BACON

This recipe must have been concocted by someone who had no other meat in the house and many mouths to feed. It's so good, I wish I had thought it up.

1/2 pound sliced bacon, cut into
*   1-inch pieces*
1 cup chopped onion
1 4-ounce can mushrooms
1 tablespoon butter
1 12-ounce package spaghetti
1 cup shredded Cheddar cheese
3 egg yolks, lightly whipped
Salt and pepper

In a skillet, over medium heat, fry bacon until crisp. Lift out and drain on paper towel. Pour off grease, return 2 tablespoonfuls to the skillet and sauté the onions in it for 5 minutes. Then put mushrooms, bacon pieces and sautéed onions into a bowl. Set aside.

Wipe the skillet, add the butter and set aside. Cook the spaghetti as the package directs.

Place the skillet over low heat and melt the cheese into the butter. Add the onion-mushroom-bacon mixture and stir well. Add cooked and well-drained spaghetti and toss to coat it evenly with the sauce. Now add the beaten egg yolks while turning the spaghetti. When it's well coated, the spaghetti is ready to serve.

Yield: 4 servings. Add fresh garlic bread to the meal. *Viva la bacon!*

SPAGHETTI la SURPLUS

Earlier I mentioned the overproductive zucchini plants in last summer's garden. I admit to being a little overproductive, myself, in freezing the vegetable for winter storage. Ever since, I've searched for ways to reduce the number of packages. That's how this recipe was born.

1/2 pound spaghetti, cooked as
*   directed on package*
1/2 cup butter or margarine,
*   divided*
4 cups zucchini, halved lengthwise
*   and then sliced into 1/2-inch*
*   pieces*
1/2 teaspoon salt
Pepper to taste
1 cup heavy cream
4 slices ham, cut in very thin
*   julienne strips*
1 cup Parmesan cheese, divided

Melt 2 tablespoons of the butter in a large skillet. Sauté zucchini over medium heat until tender but firm. Season with salt and pepper.

Add cooked and well-drained spaghetti and toss to coat it thoroughly. Use extra butter as needed. Add cream and continue to toss. Add the ham and half the Parmesan cheese and toss one last time.

Heap onto a serving dish, sprinkle with the remaining cheese. Amply serves 4 an unusually good meal. *Viva la surplus!*

ANCHOR RIVER BREAD

The other day I remembered a lunch I shared with friends many years ago on the banks of the Anchor River near Homer. We ate rounds of canned Boston brown bread.

The memory sent me to Mother's recipe files and into the kitchen, down on my knees, to look for the pressure cooker . . . not to pray. To make this recipe you must have a pressure cooker with an insert for making steamed puddings.

2 cups whole-wheat flour
1 cup all-purpose flour
1 teaspoon baking powder
1 teaspoon salt
2 eggs, lightly beaten
2/3 cup dark molasses
2 tablespoons melted butter
1 cup buttermilk
1 teaspoon baking soda
1 cup raisins, seedless or seeded

In a large mixing bowl combine the dry ingredients — the flours, baking powder and salt.

In a smaller bowl combine the lightly beaten eggs, molasses and melted butter.

In a separate bowl combine buttermilk and baking soda and mix well.

Beating in egg and buttermilk mixtures alternately, a small amount at a time, combine liquid and dry ingredients. Beat vigorously until the batter is smooth. Then fold in raisins.

Next grease the steamed pudding mold well and pour the batter into the mold. Add 3 cups water to the pressure cooker and slide the mold into the cooker. It should rest on the lowest rack. Secure the lid but do not attach the pressure control. Set the cooker on medium heat and let the steam escape for about 30 minutes.

Then add the pressure control and bring the pressure up to 15 pounds by increasing the heat. Maintain this pressure for 15 minutes. Reduce pressure, remove the lid and invert the mold on a wire rack to cool. After 20 minutes, unmold the bread and continue cooling.

It is best served cold and firm with lots of butter.

RED, WHITE & BLUE

CHAPTER 5

I'm a patriot from way back, but it isn't the flag this set of recipes brings to mind, but rather red *noses*, white *skin* and blue *berries*.

There are many dangers to be found in the average blueberry patch. It might be occupied by a bear, for example, or other dangerous and tempting fauna.

My memory of a dangerous blueberry patch goes back to when I was fifteen, big, strong and naïve. She was eighteen, small and delectable. She had needed an escort for an expedition to a berry patch . . . and my own mother loaned me to her. Now you know where I got the naïveté.

Mae had the wheels and the driver's license that transported us to the Matanuska Valley from Anchorage (and you're as naïve as I was if you believe that name). We became better acquainted on the drive. I sat next to her, casting sidelong glances at her fantastic legs.

Not once did I question her taking those legs into a mosquito-infested berry patch until we stopped, and the first bug drained its quota of blood. Then I found myself wishing Mae had worn slacks.

I splashed myself with bug dope from my private stock and offered her the jar. Back in those days we each made our own bug dope. Mine was a mixture of citronella and Vicks VapoRub. It had a strong but refreshing odor, I thought. Mae took one sniff and passed.

Since I took my job seriously, I led the way to the bear patch — I mean berry patch — a brave picture, indeed, with a rifle in my arms, determined expression on my face, and a cloud of bug dope in my wake.

I had hardly covered the bottom of my berry bucket when the mountain breeze ended, and mosquitoes descended upon us in fierce numbers. Mae suddenly asked for some bug dope. I held out the jar but she didn't take it. Would I apply the dope so her hands would stay clean? Always a gentleman, I complied.

Leaning down to catch a spot behind her ear, I found her lips only inches from mine. Suddenly her berry-picking hands were in my hair. She pulled me down and kissed me on the lips. I valiantly fought the battle to keep my bug-doped hands off her dress. Then her mouth opened in the kiss and . . . I gathered her into my arms.

When the embrace passed into phase two, breathing, she said, "I should have worn slacks. The mosquitoes are eating me alive. Will you put bug dope on my legs?"

By this time the breeze had returned and there wasn't a mosquito in sight, but one doesn't argue with a lady. Especially a lady who has nice, long legs.

We returned to Anchorage quite late and with only a few berries. I can still hear Mae explaining our bad luck to my mother, "We spent all our time rubbing on bug dope and just couldn't get any berries picked!"

Somewhere I still have that old bug-dope jar. To unscrew the cap is to relive my youth!

SUNSHINE CORN BREAD

The men building The Alaska Railroad demonstrated some imagination when it came to naming section stations on the line. Besides Honolulu, Colorado, Kashwitna and Talkeetna, there is little old Sunshine. I love sunshine. When you bake this bread you'll see how it got its name.

No two cooks use the same recipe for corn bread. In fact, with my mother, no two corn breads were alike. We got a new treat every time she baked. I follow in her footsteps with this somewhat unusual recipe.

1 cup corn meal
1 tablespoon baking powder
1 cup shredded Cheddar cheese
2 eggs
1/2 cup vegetable oil
1 cup sour cream
1 8-ounce can cream-style corn
1 8-ounce can green chilies,
*   drained and chopped*

In a large bowl, combine corn meal, baking powder and shredded cheese. In a smaller bowl, beat the eggs, add oil, sour cream, corn and green chilies. Mix well and add to dry ingredients. Stir until moistened. Spoon into a well-greased Bundt pan.

Bake at 400° for 45 minutes. When done, let cool 10 minutes before removing from pan.

SHILLELAGH BREAD

Because a loaf of Irish soda bread can turn out as hard and dangerous as an Irish shillelagh, we have named this recipe for the famous weapon. The bread isn't supposed to be hard, but it is firm enough to exercise the jaw muscles and toughen the teeth.

This isn't my Irish mother's recipe. I tried hers and learned why she didn't make soda bread. I've collected others over the years. This is the best.

1-1/2 cups whole-wheat flour
1 cup all-purpose flour
2 teaspoons sugar
1 teaspoon baking soda
1 teaspoon baking powder
1/2 cup vegetable shortening
1/2 cup raisins
3/4 cup milk
3 tablespoons vinegar
Additional milk for glaze

In a large bowl combine the flours, sugar, baking soda and baking powder. Cut in shortening until the mixture looks like bread crumbs. Mix in raisins.

In a second bowl combine milk and vinegar and pour into the flour mixture, stirring with a fork until the dry ingredients are moistened. Turn out onto a floured surface.

Knead the ball of dough gently, place it on a greased cookie sheet and flatten it to 1-1/2 inches thick. With a sharp knife crisscross the top of the loaf at 90-degree angles. Brush the top with milk to glaze.

Bake in a preheated 400° oven for 15 minutes. Reduce the heat to 375° for another 30 minutes. Then tap the bread with your fingers. If it sounds hollow, it is done. Set the finished loaf on a wire rack to cool.

The memory of that smell turns my attention to noses. Red noses in fact. All my life I have heard derogatory remarks about people who have red noses. How often we hear somebody exclaim, "Boy! Has he got a boozer's nose!" Or maybe, "His nose lights his way into every bar in town!" Or, with a childish giggle, "Daddy! Look at that man with the red nose!"

I must admit that as a trooper I jumped to conclusions about the red-nosed gentlemen I had occasion to meet. But I know that the volume of alcohol consumed is not always reflected in the nose and vice versa. A red nose *could* indicate a skin disorder.

Last Christmas as I sat in my favorite chair with my grandson, Gordy, he looked me right in the eye and said, "You have a red nose, just like Santa, Grandpa!"

Grandaughter Maria ran over to confirm his observation, "You do, Grandpa! You do!"

So who wants to cure a skin condition that fascinates grandchildren? I'll drink to that!

As to what the white of "red, white and blue" reminds me of, take your choice — this paper, the flour in the recipes, legs. . . . Off to the kitchen!

AVAILABILITY
BREAD

In my files are dozens of recipes for breads using fruits, nuts and even vegetables . . . ten recipes for zucchini bread, alone. But Harry T., the chef, taught me how to whip out every one of them using one basic recipe. His instructions were to use any fruit or vegetable that sounds good and that can be grated or mashed to measure 2 cups. Try the recipe yourself.

3 cups all-purpose flour
1/2 teaspoon baking powder
1 teaspoon salt
1 teaspoon baking soda
2 teaspoons ground cinnamon
1 cup chopped nuts
3 eggs
1-1/2 cups sugar
1 cup vegetable oil
1 teaspoon vanilla
2 cups chopped, grated or mashed
    fruit or vegetable pulp
    (see suggestions below)

In a mixing bowl combine the flour, baking powder, salt, baking soda, cinnamon and nuts.

In a second bowl beat the eggs and blend in the sugar and oil. Add vanilla and the 2 cups of fruit or vegetable pulp.

Combine both mixtures and stir until the batter is evenly moist. Divide between 2 well-greased 9 x 5-inch loaf pans.

Bake in a preheated oven at 350° for 1 hour. Test by inserting a toothpick in the center of the loaf. If it comes out clean, the bread's done. Remove loaf from the oven and let stand 10 minutes. Then remove it from the pan to finish cooling on a wire rack. You now have the makings for 2 good mug-ups.*

Some suggestions for a variety of breads:

Zucchini bread — Shred the zucchini coarsely and pack tightly into a 2-cup measure.

Orange bread — You'll need 4 large oranges. Grate a tablespoon of peel and place it in a 2-cup measure. Peel the oranges, discarding the white membrane and seeds. Finely chop the orange meat and pack it into the 2-cup measure.

Apple bread — You'll need 3 or 4 large apples. Peel, core and shred apples to fill the 2-cup measure. Add 1 teaspoon of lemon juice.

*See page 146.

MATANUSKA
(Kinda' English)
MUFFINS

In my youth English muffins and crumpets were items you read about in books. Things only the English ate with jam and marmalade at "tea," a ceremony much the same as our Alaska mug-up.*

A few years ago I watched a camp cook turn out something he called English muffins, but he cooked the darn things on top of the stove, not in the oven. I was fascinated by both the cooking and the eating. Yes, I managed to get his recipe and since have found others. I'm going to offer you a combination of ideas that deserve their own title. I hope Matanuska Muffins work for you.

6 cups all-purpose flour, divided
2 teaspoons salt
1 package active dry yeast
2 tablespoons honey or sugar
1-2/3 cups milk
1/4 cup water
1 tablespoon butter or margarine
1 egg
1/2 cup corn meal

For this recipe I use a heavy-duty electric mixer, although a large bowl and a strong arm will do the job.

Into a big bowl place 2 cups of flour, the salt and yeast. Then combine the honey, milk, water and butter in a saucepan and place over medium heat. Gradually warm the contents to very warm, approximately 115°. Slowly pour the warm liquid into the flour while beating at medium speed. Continue beating 2 to 3 minutes. Then beat at high speed for another minute. Add the egg and another cup of flour while beating at medium again. Reduce the speed and add enough flour to form a soft dough.

Turn the dough out onto a floured surface and knead until elastic and smooth. Add flour as needed. Cover with a cloth and let rise for an hour, or until double in size. Punch down and let rise again to double, about another 45 minutes.

While the dough is rising, find or make a muffin cutter that will cut a

*See page 146.

circle about 3-1/2 inches across. I have made cutters out of sheet metal or just cut both ends out of a tin can. A flat, 12-1/2-ounce tuna can or a No. 2½ can (1 lb. 13 oz.), either one, will do.

Sprinkle half the corn meal on a cookie sheet. Roll the dough to 1/2 inch thick and begin cutting circles. Place the rounds on the cookie sheet and sprinkle tops with more corn meal. Cover with a cloth and let rise for 45 minutes.

If your stove has a built-in griddle, set it on low and place the rounds on the griddle. Cook the rounds for 8 to 10 minutes on each side. If you do not have a griddle, use a large, lightly greased frying pan, and bake 4 muffins at a time. When done, they should sound hollow when tapped.

Let them cool on a rack. Eat them as you like, split, heaped with butter, strawberry jam or good cheese. For breakfast add a slice of cheese, a slice of ham and a fried egg. Sound familiar? Like Ronald's favorite breakfast?

RED NOSE BREAD

I have an "older friend" who claims he is going to live to be at least 150, but he will not tell me how far he has to go. This ambition isn't the only factor that distinguishes him from his peers. He possesses one of the grandest red noses around. It is not a Rudolph red, but closer to dying-ember red. Ah, heck! It's a boozer's nose.

Every holiday I take him a loaf of mincemeat-banana bread. If his reaction is any indication, the recipe will win a million converts to this way of using fine brandy.

1/4 cup brandy (the good stuff, please)
1 9-ounce package condensed mincemeat
3 cups all-purpose flour
1 tablespoon baking powder
1 teaspoon salt
1/2 cup milk
1/2 cup dark corn syrup
1/4 cup sugar
1 egg
1/4 cup vegetable oil
1 cup ripe bananas, peeled and mashed

In a small bowl combine brandy and mincemeat, breaking it up so that it absorbs all the brandy.

In a medium bowl combine flour, baking powder and salt. Mix well.

In a larger bowl combine milk, corn syrup, sugar, egg, oil and mashed banana. Mix these ingredients well and add the mincemeat. Mix well again.

Now add the flour mixture and stir thoroughly. When everything is well mixed, spread batter into a well-greased, or nonstick bread pan.

Bake at 350° for 75 minutes, or until a toothpick inserted at the center comes out clean.

Cool in the pan for 10 minutes before removing from pan. Place on a cake rack to finish cooling. This bread will keep a couple of weeks if it is well wrapped and refrigerated, and it makes a nice gift even for a non-red-nosed friend.

WILD BLUEBERRY RING

I've already mentioned one reason I like blueberries. Maybe you could call it a one-time fringe benefit that is hard to forget. But enough of that. I've eaten wild Alaskan blueberries all my life. The blue tongues of the youth of the state indicate that's one taste that hasn't changed.

To reduce my many blueberry recipes to one entry was difficult, but here is my offering:

1/2 cup warm water, 105° to 115°
1 tablespoon active dry yeast
2-1/2 cups all-purpose flour
3 tablespoons sugar
1/2 teaspoon salt
6 tablespoons butter or margarine
2 eggs, separated
1/2 cup milk
1/2 cup brown sugar
1 teaspoon finely grated orange
      peel
2 cups fresh blueberries
1 teaspoon cinnamon

In a small bowl dissolve the yeast in warm water and set aside to start bubbling.

In a large mixing bowl combine flour, sugar and salt. Then cut in butter until pieces are the size of peas.

Separate the eggs and set the whites to one side. Combine the yolks, milk and the dissolved yeast.

Add this liquid to the flour mixture and stir until dry ingredients are moistened. Form into a ball, cover and chill for at least 4 hours. The dough can be held overnight, if you wish to have the blueberry ring for breakfast.

When you are ready to proceed, knead the dough lightly on a floured surface. Then roll into a rectangle about 12 x 20 inches.

Next beat the egg whites until soft peaks form. Stir in 2 tablespoons brown sugar and the orange peel. Spread this mixture evenly over the surface of the flattened dough. Sprinkle on remaining brown sugar, blueberries and cinnamon.

Roll the dough up like a jelly roll. Pinch the edges to seal. Ease the roll into a 10-inch tube pan that is well greased. Brush the top with butter and sprinkle on a little white sugar.

Slide into a preheated 375° oven for 35 minutes or until lightly browned. Cool for 15 minutes; remove from the pan. Finish cooling on a wire rack.

Serve either slightly warm or cold. Try it on a Sunday morning, even if you have to use frozen blueberries. You'll enjoy!

FRENCHIE'S BREAD ORDINAIRE

My friend Frenchie works hard to be memorable and succeeds. He has a number of famous sayings . . . if repetition can make sayings famous. One he likes is, "All women should know a Frenchman at least once in their lives!" To which I respond, "So they'll know by the contrast when they later find a real man!" We disagree rather often.

Another favorite saying is, "I'm the only Frenchman in the state who knows how to make true French bread *ordinaire.*" With this statement I must agree. Only when Frenchie learned that my grandmother was French did he consent to show me his method. Now, it's *our* method:

2 packages active dry yeast
2-1/2 cups warm water,
　　105° to 115°
6 cups all-purpose flour
1 teaspoon salt

Stir yeast into warm water in a large bowl and let stand 5 minutes until bubbly.

Beating constantly, add flour, a half-cup at a time, until you have 4 cups of flour in the mixture and it is smooth. Dissolve salt in a small amount of water and beat into the batter.

Add enough more flour to form a soft dough and turn out onto a floured surface. Knead the dough, adding flour, if necessary, to keep it from sticking.

Clean the bowl and grease the inside. Form dough into a ball and return to the bowl. Turn the dough once to bring greased surface to the top and cover the bowl with a towel or other cloth. Place the dough in a warm area and let it rise until it triples in size. This usually takes 2 hours.

Punch down the dough, knead briefly, and let rise again to three

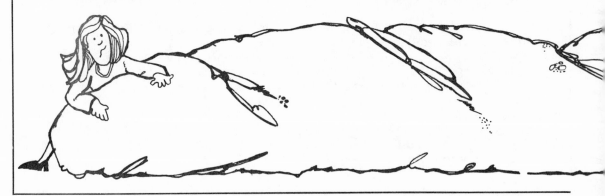

times the original size, about another 1-1/2 hours.

Turn the dough out onto a floured surface and cut it into 4 equal pieces. Shape each piece into a long roll, slightly tapered at the ends. Each should be 16 to 18 inches long. Place the loaves on a large cookie sheet — or maybe two cookie sheets. Do not let loaves touch; keep well apart to allow expansion. Let them rise in a warm place until doubled in size. Slash each loaf diagonally about 4 times, 1/4 inch deep.

On the bottom shelf of your oven place a shallow pan for water. Preheat oven to 450°. Five minutes before placing loaves in the oven add a cup of water to the pan. The resulting moisture develops this bread's distinctive crust.

Bake the loaves in the middle of the oven for 25 minutes or until golden brown. Finished bread should sound hollow when tapped with the finger.

Slide the baked loaves onto a wire rack to cool. Five minutes later, if you must (and I nearly always must), you can try a warm loaf. Slice it in wide slices, dab on butter thickly, and top it with a slice of good cheese. Frenchie's Bread *Ordinaire, c'est extraordinaire!*

SKWENTNA FLATBREAD

Skwentna used to be a FAA (Federal Aviation Agency) station north and west of Anchorage. Today it's a school. I last visited the place on official trooper business, a case of cabin fever that had to be cured before anyone was killed over it.

Later, when I was standing on the runway, waiting for a plane, a woman waved a coffee cup at me, the universal Alaskan invitation for a mug-up.* She served me this flatbread:

2-1/2 cups warm water, 105°
to 115°
1 tablespoon active dry yeast
3 tablespoons molasses
1 tablespoon butter or margarine
2 teaspoons finely grated orange
peel
1-1/2 teaspoons salt
1-1/2 cups rye flour
2 tablespoons soy flour
2-1/2 cups all-purpose flour

In a large mixing bowl, dissolve the yeast in warm water. Stir in 1 tablespoon of molasses and let stand until bubbly.

Then stir in the rest of the molasses, butter, orange peel, salt, rye and soy flours. Beat until the mixture is smooth. Stir in 2 cups all-purpose flour and add just enough more to make a stiff dough.

*See page 146.

Turn onto a floured surface and knead until elastic and smooth, approximately 10 minutes.

Form into a ball and place in a well-greased bowl, turn once and cover. Let rise in a warm place until doubled, about 1 hour.

Punch down the dough and form again into a round loaf. Then flatten it to 1 inch thick. Place on a cookie sheet and let rise another 45 minutes to double in size.

Bake in a preheated 375° oven for about 30 minutes or until the bread makes a hollow sound when it's thumped. Cool on a wire rack.

This bread is good hot, warm or cold, with lots of butter and jam.

LOUENDOWSKI'S BABKA BREAD
with Cinnamon Topping

Way back during World War II, I spent a couple of years with a guy named Louendowski, whom we called "Lu." He was big, tough, Polish and proud of it. One of the things he longed for while in Alaska was *babka*, which he described as a sweet bread, more like cake. He had me drooling when he described the rum sauce served with it.

At last someone sent me a recipe for *babka*. I have named it for Lu.

1 cup milk
1/4 cup water
1 package active dry yeast
1/2 cup sugar
1 teaspoon salt
1/2 cup butter
4 whole eggs
1 extra egg yolk
4-1/2 cups sifted all-purpose flour
1/2 cup seedless raisins

Heat milk slowly in a saucepan until bubbles form around the edges. Then add the water. Check the temperature. It must be between 105° and 115°. Then remove mixture from heat and sprinkle yeast over the surface, stirring until it dissolves. Pour into a large mixing bowl and wait 5 minutes.

Add in sugar, salt, butter, eggs and egg yolk. Beat until blended. Add 3 cups of the flour and beat until smooth. Add another 1-1/2 cups of flour and beat until the dough leaves the sides of the bowl. Mix in the raisins and cover with a cloth. Set in a warm place to rise for an hour. Dough should double in size.

For baking use a 6-quart Dutch oven. Line the bottom and sides with aluminum foil. Turn dough into the pan and let rise for another hour.

You could bake the loaf right now and have a fine bread, but a cinnamon topping goes well with it, too. Besides, it will use your extra egg white.

Cinnamon Topping
1 egg white
1 tablespoon water
2 tablespoons all-purpose flour
2 tablespoons sugar
2 tablespoons butter
1/2 teaspoon cinnamon

Just before you bake the loaf, brush the top with a mixture of egg white and 1 tablespoon of water. Then combine the flour, sugar, butter and cinnamon and sprinkle it over the top.

Bake in a preheated 350° oven for 1 hour or until a cake tester comes out clean. Set pan on a rack for 15 minutes. Then lift out the bread and foil. Peel off the foil.

Serve the bread in wedges with lots of butter. Or go all out and pass the strawberry jam or rum sauce.

CHINIAK
FLANK ROLL

The easternmost point of land on Kodiak Island is called Cape Chiniak. It's the last thing you see as you leave the island headed south.

I first saw it as a boy aboard a cannery tender named *Smile* and last saw it from a patrol car window. The large, hairy, reddish-colored beef cattle that roam the area impressed me the most.

A few years later I had a chance to buy some meat from the cape. One piece I obtained was a nice flank steak. This is how I cooked it:

3 pounds flank steak, beef or moose
1/2 cup finely chopped celery
1 clove garlic, minced
1 15-ounce can tomatoes, broken
    into small pieces
2 cups beef stock (or 3 bouillon
    cubes and 2 cups water)
1 teaspoon cumin
1 teaspoon rosemary, crumbled
1 teaspoon salt
1 tablespoon dried parsley
1 12-ounce can beer
1 cup chopped onion, divided
3 tablespoons vegetable oil

Your first act is to have the butcher tie the meat into a roll. Or do it yourself. Roll it with the grain and tie securely in 3 or 4 places along its length. Put the roll into a baking pan. I use the 13 x 9 x 2-inch size.

Next we'll need a marinade. In a mixing bowl combine celery, garlic, tomatoes, stock, cumin, rosemary, salt, parsley, beer and 1/2 cup of the chopped onions. Pour the mixture over the meat and roll the meat around in it. Cover the pan with aluminum foil and marinate it overnight in a cool place (35° to 40°). Turn it several times if possible. (If you're in a hurry, marinate for at least 4 hours.)

Drain the meat, saving the marinade, and pat it dry with paper towel. Heat oil in a large frying pan and brown the meat roll on all sides over medium heat.

Now put the meat back in the marinade, cover with foil and bake at 350° for 2 hours. Try to baste the meat with the pan juices every half-hour.

Meanwhile, in the frying pan, sauté the remaining onions and spoon these over the roast during the last half-hour of its cooking time.

Remove the roast to a cutting board. Put the roasting pan on top of the stove and boil the liquid, uncovered, until it is reduced by a third.

Slice the meat and arrange on a serving platter. Drizzle some of the sauce over the meat slices and serve the rest in a gravy boat.

MOOSE ROULETTE

CHAPTER 6

Back in the days when I went crashing through the woods each fall in search of the wily moose, I had lots of fun, quickly followed, usually, by a large helping of hard work. Only after field butchering, packing out, cutting into eating size pieces and freezing the beast I'd won did the fun begin again . . . when I could cook and eat this delicious meat. More about the eating later.

I remember my father's sage advice when I was about to engage in my first hunt, "A moose is where you find him, lad." With that, I ventured forth into the wilds of Alaska. I found nothing.

The following week I joined forces with another young man. While he had never actually found a moose of his own, either, he had been on several successful hunts. He had even seen one lying dead in the woods. As no one could have dragged the animal to that spot, he at least knew where a moose had once been. Back to this same spot we sneaked.

Wet and miserable after soaking up the pre-dawn dew, we arrived at a low hilltop overlooking a dish-shaped valley some 400 yards across. My partner assured me a moose had to be bedded down in that valley. I was to stay put while he circled around.

With the coming of dawn, a light mist began to rise from the floor of the valley. Within minutes it was high and dense enough that a moose would have had to be ten feet tall to show above it. Then I felt a whiff of wind at my back and I stood, rifle in hand, waiting for the breeze to blow a hole in the mist.

Suddenly a dark hulk rose out of the misty brush not thirty feet from where I stood. I felt the hair on the back of my neck try to stand up. The hulk turned and the semi-ugly head of a moose, with about four-foot antlers, looked me right in the eye. The light wind must have carried my scent to him.

We stared at each other a long fifteen

seconds before I remembered that I was moose hunting, lifted the rifle, found my point of aim and squeezed the trigger. A great "Ba-loom!" of sound filled the valley. The moose was well hit. It turned around, took one step and crumpled in a heap.

I'll always remember my first impression walking up to that dead animal. "My God! What have I done?" I thought. I knew the two of us would never be able to pack out an animal this huge.

My hunting partner, arriving at the kill out of breath, managed to gasp, "You sure ruined the day's hunting, Gordy!" He was so right. We worked like slaves getting that animal out of the woods.

M̲oose hunting can be both fun and profitable. It is when the moose hunts you

HIGHBUSH MOOSE POT ROAST

As I explained in my first cookbook, *LOWBUSH MOOSE,* the big, ugly, hairy creatures with the antlers are the real highbush moose. Lowbush moose are arctic hare or rabbit.

Likewise, cranberries grow on two levels in Alaska, highbush and lowbush. (You can guess where this is taking us.) You want the meat from the high bush and the berries from the low one for this dish. Or go buy a boneless rolled beef roast (as I did) and whatever fresh cranberries you can find.

4 pounds boneless rolled roast,
     beef or highbush moose
2 tablespoons vegetable oil
2 tablespoons all-purpose flour
1-1/2 teaspoons salt
Pepper to taste
1-1/2 cups beef stock (or 4 bouillon
     cubes and 1-1/2 cups water)
2 cups chopped onion
2 cups fresh cranberries, lowbush
     or bog cranberry preferred

The 6-quart Dutch oven is the tool for this job. Set it on medium heat and add the oil. Wipe the meat with a damp cloth and rub on a mixture of flour, salt and pepper. Brown the meat on all sides.

Remove the meat from the pan and discard the pan drippings. Add the stock, onions and cranberries to the pan. Return the meat to the pan, bring to a boil and reduce the heat to a simmer for 2-1/2 hours. Turn the meat once or twice during the cooking. When it's tender, remove it from the liquid and onto a platter. Cover and keep warm.

Skim the excess fat off the liquid in the pan. Pour the liquid into a blender, blend for 1 minute; then pour it through a strainer back into the pan. Reheat and add seasoning if needed.

Slice the roast and arrange it on a platter. Pour the sauce over the meat and serve the rest in a gravy boat. Be sure to serve something else with the meat that demands gravy, too. Serves 8 or more.

that the fun and profit stop or, worse, run to danger and expense. Alaskan moose have adapted a game that should have been left with the Russians. It is known as "moose roulette," and it is played out against man's most expensive (and dangerous) toy, the automobile.

Let's say I am blasting down the highway on a moonlit winter night, traveling slightly above reasonable speed because the road surface seems good. Only a few icy spots. The headlights are on high. I am in full control.

Then a shadow appears far down the roadway. I lift my foot from the gas pedal and the vehicle's nose drops slightly. The lights pick up the glint of animal eyes, but they are too close to the ground to be moose eyes. As I watch, the eyes begin to move up. The animal jumps onto the road and, suddenly, the eyes are moose height and straight in front of me. Moose roulette time!

I slow down and move to the left lane. But he's crossing to the left side of the road, so I return to the right. Relief passes through me. I'm going to make it by.

The animal is now easily visible in the headlights. He's almost to the left shoulder when I see him plant his feet and swing to

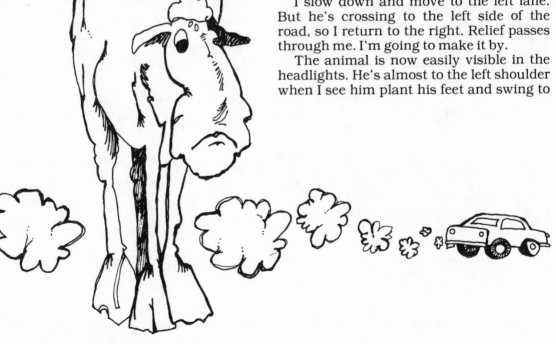

CURRY CURRIED MOOSE

One of the wide spots along The Alaska Railroad used to be Curry. I visited there three times, once on a ski trip, which resulted in a large group of sore muscles and a fuzzy memory of the return train ride.

The second time I flew in to investigate deaths in a fire that burned the hotel down. I earned sore muscles that time, too, when I had to push an airplane up onto the top of the snow so we could get it going on its skis.

But I didn't know what sore muscles were until the third and last time I visited Curry when I managed to take a moose and had to pack it home. At least I enjoyed part of that animal in the following recipe.

*2 pounds beef or moose chuck
    steak, sliced across the grain
    in 1/8-inch-thick pieces
2 tablespoons vegetable oil
2 cups chopped onion
1 teaspoon salt
2 tablespoons curry powder
2 cups water, divided
2 tablespoons flour
1 cup cooked, sliced carrots*

Place your 6-quart Dutch oven on medium heat and add the oil. Cook the meat, stirring often, until well browned. I usually do only half at a time. Remove the meat.

Sauté the onions in the pan until slightly browned. Add the salt and curry powder and mix well.

Return the meat to the pan and add 1-1/2 cups of water. Bring to a boil, reduce heat and simmer for 1-1/2 hours, or until the meat is tender. Combine the flour with 1/2 cup cold water and stir into the liquid. Continue cooking until the liquid thickens into a sauce. Add carrots and heat for another 2 minutes.

Serve with rice or noodles. The dish will serve 6 with ease.

his right for another crack at moose roulette.

I stand on the brakes and try unsuccessfully not to close my eyes. I count one, two, three . . . and there is a light "Thump!" on the front of the car. The car stops with a jerk. My eyes snap open. No moose in sight. In a flash I am out looking for damage. It is only a dent in the headlight rim. I'm lucky.

From behind comes the clatter of hoofs. I wheel around just in time to let the moose push my outstretched arm with his shoulder. His lumbering weight drives me into the most nearly perfect pirouette I've ever executed.

Have you seen a moose grin? This one grins from out of the darkness there at the far side of the road. Not wanting to play any more, I make a dash for the car, pour on the gas and plan to outrun him for the next mile.

Fantasy? Not altogether and, unfortunately, Alaska's highway statistics show that the biggest departure from reality may be the part where I come out of a game of moose roulette uninjured.

The moose has another trait besides playfulness that makes him dangerous. He prefers the beaten path. I offer, as an example, the path between my big house and the little house out back. No, not the renter's place. The outhouse. The trail between these two structures is usually the first one shoveled out after a snow, sometimes at odd hours of the night.

One cold clear night — in fact, a night so cold that trips out are made only on an emergency basis — I pulled on my pants and stepped out onto the path.

I was three steps out the door when I became aware of a large brown blob in the

BOATING BEEF

Down in Southeastern Alaska we suffered many early season fishing trips. We loved to fish so much that we went out before there were fish. Some of our friends were honest enough to call them "boating trips." One such expedition brought this recipe to my attention.

3 pounds round steak, beef or
*   moose, cut into 1/4-inch-thick*
*   slices about 3 inches long*
1/4 cup soy sauce
1/2 cup minced onion
1/2 cup salad oil
2 cloves garlic, minced
1 teaspoon sesame oil
2 teaspoons sugar
1/2 teaspoon ground ginger

Mix everything except the meat in a large bowl. Add the meat, cover and refrigerate for 4 to 8 hours. Or pour the marinade over the meat in a sturdy plastic bag and seal it well if you are planning to take it aboard your boat.

This meat is best charcoal grilled either in your backyard or on your boat's "over-the-side" barbecue grill.

Grill the little strips of meat a minute on each side and serve with the rest of your meal. You'll wish you had prepared more, but this amount will serve 4 nicely.

The backyard cooking does eliminate seasickness.

trail ahead of me. It had to be a moose. Sensible bears were asleep for the winter. I moved ahead with every intention of bluffing the moose, a female, from my outhouse trail.

She matched me step for step from the other direction. Clearly, she was inviting me to step right out in the deep snow and let her pass.

But that night my feet were encased in the rubber bottoms cut out of an old pair of Shoe-Pacs — my "go-to-the-nushnik" slippers — not exactly snow wading equipment. The big old cow moose was better equipped.

I elected to stubborn her out by jumping up and down and yelling. Then I ran like hell for the outhouse door, the cow breathing down my neck most of the way. I slammed the door in her face or she would have joined me inside. When I next peeked out, she was gone.

Making a run for the house, I was halfway back when the sound of pounding hoofs came from behind. I beat her to the door by only one step.

Male, female, playful or stubborn, I prefer my moose as meat on the table. You will, too, if you try some of my recipes.

HEINE HOMINY BEEF

Over the years I have discovered that I am part of a minority. It is made up of those lucky few who have palates capable of appreciating the delicate taste of man's most fascinating adaptation of the corn kernel. Yes, hominy!

I have to be extremely sneaky to get the other members of my family to eat it. At Heine Creek, up in the interior of Alaska, I achieved one of my little known but major triumphs. I slipped hominy to my family in this recipe:

1 pound lean ground beef or moose
1 tablespoon vegetable oil
1-1/2 cups chopped onion
1 chopped green pepper
3 cloves garlic, minced
1/2 teaspoon salt
1/4 teaspoon pepper
1 teaspoon dried basil
1 teaspoon dried parsley
1 pinch cayenne
1 8-ounce can kidney beans with
    liquid
1 15-ounce can golden hominy
    (Delicious!)

In a large frying pan brown the meat in the oil over medium heat. When browned, add the onions, green pepper and garlic, stirring all the time. When these are tender, add the salt, pepper and other spices. Stir well and add the beans and hominy. Cook for 10 minutes more. Serve in deep bowls with lots of good bread.

WHITE CUBE MEAT LOAF

Back in our days of many mouths to feed on a limited income, we developed some interesting recipes to make the available meat go farther. Hash was a popular way of stretching the meat supply so eight people could eat well. We even had spruce hen hash once. Another way was to add cubes of potatoes to the meat loaf.

Recently one of my daughters, in her twenties now, asked me why I didn't make the white cube meat loaf anymore. She remembered the dish fondly, and that was nice to hear. Maybe you would like to try the recipe.

2 cups potatoes — boiled 15
        minutes, cooled, cubed in
        1/4-inch pieces
2 pounds ground beef or moose
2 eggs, beaten
1 8-ounce can tomato sauce
1 cup chopped onion
1 clove garlic, minced fine
1/4 cup finely chopped celery
1-1/2 teaspoons salt
1/4 teaspoon pepper
1 cup bread crumbs
1 teaspoon rosemary, crumbled
6 slices bacon, 4 inches long

In a large mixing bowl combine the meat, eggs, tomato sauce, onions, garlic, celery, salt, pepper, bread crumbs and rosemary. Mix well. Get right into it with both (clean) hands. Then mix in the potato cubes by hand as well. Shape the meat into an oval loaf not over 3 inches thick in a 13 x 9 x 2-inch baking pan. Lay the sliced bacon across the top.

Slide into a 350° oven for 1-1/2 hours. When done remove to the cutting board and let stand for 10 minutes to firm up for cutting. Slice and arrange slices on a serving platter.

We often served *more* potatoes with the meat loaf, but rice is a good, filling accompaniment, too. May your children remember the dish as fondly as mine do.

FOWL FRIED FLANK

The earlier cafes, restaurants and roadhouses in Alaska seldom bothered to keep well-aged and well-cut steaks on hand. Instead they had lots of just plain beef and a heavy pounding mallet to turn out something they called "Chicken fried steak." Usually it was good.

When I began butchering my own moose for the freezer, I found myself with a lot of strange cuts of meat. In a flash of inspiration, I labeled them "breakfast steaks." Later, with a meat pounding hammer, I turned these tough, strange cuts into Fowl Fried Flank.

1-1/2 pounds moose or beef steak—
    flank or top round — cut 1/2
    inch thick
1 teaspoon salt
1/4 teaspoon pepper
1 tablespoon milk
1 egg
1 cup cracker crumbs
1/4 cup vegetable oil

Gravy
3 tablespoons pan drippings
2 tablespoons flour
1-1/2 cups milk
Salt and pepper

Cut the meat into serving-size pieces and pound them flat with a meat tenderizing hammer. Salt and pepper the pieces.

Mix the tablespoon of milk with the egg and beat well. Dip meat pieces into the egg mixture and then into cracker crumbs.

Heat oil in a skillet and brown both sides of the meat, a few pieces at a time. When all pieces are browned, cover the skillet and cook the meat slowly for 45 minutes. Remove meat to a platter and keep warm.

At serving time, prepare the gravy by combining hot pan drippings with flour to make a roux. Add milk slowly and stir over medium heat until gravy is thickened. Salt and pepper to taste.

Traditionally, the meat is served with gravy already poured over it, but you may wish to save some to serve in a gravy boat to accompany boiled potatoes, which are so good with this dish. Yield: 4 to 6 servings.

BEER-DRINKERS' SHORT RIBS

I have discovered that cooking dinner during the time normally reserved for watching football on TV can create a definite conflict of interests. Besides interrupting the game, it interferes with the beer drinking. In my constant effort to solve problems (my own), the following concept of cooking has evolved. Try it on a Sunday afternoon.

1 6-pack beer (12-ounce cans)
4 pounds short ribs, beef or moose,
*   cut into 2-inch segments*
1/2 teaspoon salt
1/4 teaspoon pepper
4 onions, sliced
1/2 cup flour
1 clove garlic, minced
1 bay leaf
1/2 teaspoon dried rosemary,
*   crumbled*
3 whole cloves
Malt-flavored vinegar

Open a can of beer and set your Dutch oven on the counter. Spread the ribs out on the breadboard and salt and pepper them well. Place the flour in a paper sack and shake the meat in it, a piece or two at a time. Spread the onions over the bottom of the Dutch oven. Layer the meat over the onions. Add the garlic, bay leaf, rosemary and cloves to the top of the meat. Open another can of beer and pour over the meat. (I assume you've already drunk the first can.)

Cover the Dutch oven and slide it into a 350° oven for 3 to 3-1/2 hours (if the game goes into overtime), or until tender. While the meat is cooking, drink the remaining cans of beer. Should the Dutch oven require additional liquid during cooking, it will find water a reasonable substitute for beer.

During the last hour of cooking, try to arrange for someone else to cook some potatoes. After the game serve the ribs by removing them to a platter and sprinkling them with malt vinegar. Enjoy both food and game!

NEWHALEN MOOSE PIE

The name for this recipe comes from the village of Newhalen, down near Iliamna Lake in western Alaska. The man who gave me the recipe spent a winter near the village. The only meat he saw from August of one year to July of the next was moose. He claims to know 200 recipes for cooking moose and is writing a cookbook. He weakened enough to give me this single recipe. It's a pie, full of meat, and very good.

2 pounds stew meat, beef or moose, cut into 1-inch cubes
1/4 cup flour
1 teaspoon salt
3 tablespoons shortening or vegetable oil
1 cup chopped onion, or 1/2 cup dried flakes
1 cup carrots, sliced 1/4 inch thick
1/4 teaspoon thyme
1-1/2 cups beef stock (or 4 bouillon cubes and 1-1/2 cups water)
2 tablespoons Worcestershire (optional)
1/4 teaspoon pepper
1 stick pie crust dough (or mix your favorite dough)
1 egg, beaten

Shake the pieces of meat in a sack with the flour and salt. Add the oil or shortening to a Dutch oven and place on medium heat. Brown about half the meat at a time and remove to another dish.

When all the meat is browned return it to the Dutch oven and combine it with onions, carrots, thyme, stock, Worcestershire sauce and pepper. Bring to a boil, cover and simmer for 1-1/2 hours.

Pour the mixture into a 9 x 9-inch square baking pan and cover with a pie crust. Trim and flute the edges and pierce the crust in several places to allow steam to escape.

Brush the top with beaten egg. Bake at 425° for 25 minutes or until the crust is golden brown.

The pie will serve 4 adequately and maybe one more if a mug-up* should stay for dinner.

*See page 146.

FUNNY-TALKING MEATBALLS

Swedish meatball recipes in my files number in the dozens. No two alike. I worried about the best one to share with you and have chosen the one that came from a beautiful young Swedish woman with a strong accent and limited English. She was tall, blonde, and blue eyed, had legs that were positively fantastic . . . and she could cook. Here's her recipe.

2 slices dry bread, trimmed of crust
1/2 cup milk
1 pound ground beef, lean or
*   extra-lean*
1/2 cup minced onion
1 teaspoon salt
1/8 teaspoon pepper
1 egg, beaten
3/4 teaspoon allspice, divided
1 tablespoon vegetable oil
1/2 cup chicken stock
1/2 cup sour cream

Chop the bread into pieces and combine with milk in a medium bowl. Allow to soak for a few minutes; then add the beef, onion, salt, pepper, egg and 1/2 teaspoon of the allspice. Mix well with a heavy-duty mixer or your hands. Then with wet hands measure out tablespoon amounts and form into meatballs.

Heat a large skillet, add the oil and the meatballs. Roll them around while sautéing over medium heat until they are browned on all sides. Cook 10 minutes and remove to a clean bowl.

Pour the chicken stock into the skillet and loosen the particles of browning residue. Add the remaining allspice and the sour cream to the pan. Mix these well.

Return the meatballs to the mixture in the skillet and stir them around so all sides are coated with the sour cream mixture. Cook over medium heat for 5 minutes, but NEVER let the liquid boil.

Turn out into a serving dish and spoon sauce on top. Or serve in a chafing dish for real class. To turn meatballs into an hors d'oeuvre for a party, just stick a toothpick in each one and keep the dish warm.

MEATBALL SAGA

CHAPTER 7

The sad saga of John "Meatball" Johansen is one of early Alaska. No one knows from whence he came, and even one of my advanced age met him only when I was a boy. In our all too brief encounter, he wasn't really at his best. In fact, he was falling down drunk at the time. So why am I telling the story?

Meatball was a friend of my brother, Ken, who collected people like others collect stray cats. Meatball was my image of Ichabod Crane, the headless horseman, tall and skinny, all bones and awkwardness. And — you won't be surprised, even though I certainly was — Meatball was a cook, a special kind of cook who could turn out meals for five men or a hundred, on land or aboard ship, with equal skill.

Though he and Ken were friends earlier, the Meatball saga really begins in 1936. Ken was working at the Lucky Shot mine in the Willow Creek area of Alaska, nursemaiding a pair of stationary marine diesel engines that powered the mine. He knew

the mine had been having mess hall problems. One cook after another had come and gone in a two-month period.

The crew was rapidly approaching mutiny. The cold and the wet and other miserable working conditions they tolerated, but not bad food.

One afternoon when Ken was standing outside the engine room catching a breath of fresh mountain air, the company truck arrived from Anchorage. Out of the cab stepped Meatball Johansen. He was clean-shaven, wore a suit and had only half-bloodshot eyes. He seemed able to focus his eyes and spotted Ken but gave only a slight wave.

Ken stepped into the roadway to meet him and shouted, "Hi, Meatball!"

The answer came quickly back, "Sssh! My name's 'Johnny,' Ken! Please!"

Quick on the uptake, Ken switched to "Johnny" and arranged to get together after his shift.

It was then Meatball told Ken why he

wanted to be called Johnny. Cooking in various camps with cheap management and tight food budgets, he had served too many beans and meatballs. The nickname "Meatball" had begun to haunt him so that he had a hard time finding jobs and an even harder time keeping them. Someone always recognized him and called him "Meatball" again. He needed a chance to reestablish himself in a camp for a while without the name finding him.

The fact that Meatball was in poor physical condition must have worked on Ken's sympathy, too. The man was fighting to live as well as to live down a name.

Meatball was a good cook, well able to supervise others when he was too weak to work himself. With two bull cooks to help him, he took command of the kitchen and mess hall. Almost at once the quality of food improved. At the end of six weeks in a no-alcohol camp, the name "Meatball" seemed behind him, and he was healthy again. With these improvements came a feeling of confidence.

One Saturday night he served his famous sweet-and-sour meatballs, but a lot of the crew skipped dinner that night to catch the car headed for Anchorage, anticipating a wild and woolly night on the town.

That weekend, Ken drove the big, long, seven-passenger sedan. The driver was obligated to stay sober and round up the crew for the trip back to the mine Sunday night, a roundup that for daring and difficulty would challenge any performed on cattle. At least cattle are sober. The miners never were.

As Ken described it, there were two kinds of drunks. First were the jolly but limp type, the ones who usually got sick. Accordingly, these were placed at the bottom of the pile in the back of the car. The other type were the fighters. They

didn't want to go back to the mine but expected the driver to take them back even if he had to fight them to do it. The driver's choice was either to talk them into the car or knock them unconscious and throw them in on top of the jolly but limp drunks.

Only the soberest drunk was allowed to sit up front and help the driver fight off the other passengers. Many times the driver had to stop and reunconscious a passenger.

But I digress from the saga of Meatball. Since that Saturday dinner went well, the next Wednesday he served his famous Swedish meatballs. The nutmeg sauce and onion rings were perfect.

JENSEN MEATBALLS

This recipe came to me marked "Danish" and naturally caught my eye because my dad was so proud of his Danish background. Jensen is the name my great-grandfather wore. His son at birth was named John, Neil's son. But when John Neilson arrived in the good old USA, he dropped the "i" and became John Nelson. His son was George Nelson, and so on to me.

1 pound ground beef, or moose, or
*   half veal and half pork*
1 cup bread crumbs
1/4 cup minced onion
1 teaspoon salt
1/8 teaspoon pepper
1/8 teaspoon ground nutmeg
1 cup beef stock, divided
3 tablespoons butter, margarine or
*   vegetable oil*

In a large mixing bowl combine meat, crumbs, onion, salt, pepper, nutmeg and 1/3 cup of the beef stock. Mix well. With wet hands, form about 2 tablespoons of meat into a small, elongated meatloaf, about 1-1/2 x 2-1/2 inches. Repeat until all meat is formed in loaves, then flatten them slightly.

Brown the meat creations in butter over medium heat, turning once. Add remaining 2/3 cup stock, then reduce the heat and cook slowly for 30 minutes, turning several more times.

Serve with potatoes, rice or noodles. Yield: 4 servings.

MEATBALLS AND CABBAGE

The woman who sent this recipe said it was Bavarian, but I've never been sure what that means. A camp cook told me once, "Make it taste good, then add a few caraway seeds. That's Bavarian!" So here we are: Bavarian Meatballs and Cabbage.

1 pound ground beef or moose
1/2 cup bread crumbs
1 egg
1/4 teaspoon salt
1/2 teaspoon caraway seed
2 tablespoons vegetable oil
1 10-ounce can mushroom soup
1/2 cup water
1 3-ounce package cream cheese
1/2 cup sliced carrots
1/4 cup sliced celery
*1/4 cup green pepper, sliced in
     strips*
4 cups shredded cabbage

In a large bowl combine the meat, bread crumbs, egg, salt and half the caraway seed. Mix well with hands. With wet hands shape the meat into about 16 meatballs. Brown in oil in a large, covered skillet or Dutch oven over medium heat. Roll to brown all sides.

While meat is browning, combine soup, water, cream cheese and remaining caraway seed in a bowl and blend well.

Pour the excess fat off the meatballs, add the soup-cream cheese mixture, carrots and celery to the pan. Cover and cook for 10 minutes.

Add the green peppers and the cabbage to the pan and continue to cook for 20 more minutes, stirring several times. When the cabbage is done, the dish is ready to serve.

It will serve 4 with the taste of old Bavaria, whatever that may be.

With great personal control, Meatball didn't serve meatballs again until the following Monday, when he dished up another famed recipe, meatballs with cottage cheese. Ken noticed a miner giving Meatball a strange look that night.

Thursday brought meatballs with cabbage from the Matanuska Valley. No less a personage than the mine superintendent sent his compliments to the chef. In fact he yelled them across the mess hall, "Damned good dinner, Cook!" Everyone seemed to like the dinner.

The following Sunday evening, Ken began to suspect that Meatball had gone too far. The super had gone to town, but it was too far from payday for anyone else to go. Most of the crew was in the mess hall when Bohemian meatballs were served, complete with tomatoes, mushrooms and macaroni.

A miner in the back of the hall took one bite and jumped to his feet yelling, "It's Meatball Johansen! I thought I knew that face. We'll eat nothing but these damned meatballs from now on. Let's run him out of camp!"

A strange quiet fell over the mess hall, although the sound of forks shoveling food remained. No one jumped to support the rabble-rouser.

Still standing, the meatball-hater pointed a fork dripping Bohemian sauce at the cook and shouted, "He's got to go! If you are all scared of the super, *I'll* run Meatball out of camp!"

Into the silence that followed there came the sound of a chair scraping back from the table. Was it the signal for a general rush at Meatball? No. Sven Anderson, the night shift boss, all 255 pounds of him, had risen from his chair and stood towering over everyone in the hall.

"Now, I tell you!" Sven began. "Nobody is running anyone out of camp, except maybe me. I like what this cook makes,

ALUGNIGMUK MEATBALL CASSEROLE

If people out there can add the word Bavarian to just any old recipe, try "Alugnigmuk" on your tongue. We have some good names in Alaska too (though you won't find this one on any map). Despite the caraway seed, this dish is Alaskan. You have my permission to rename it if you absolutely have to, but never leave out the apple.

1 pound lean ground beef or moose
1/4 cup bread crumbs
1 egg
3/4 cup finely chopped onion, divided
1 teaspoon salt, divided
1/4 cup beef stock or water
2 teaspoons horseradish
1/4 teaspoon pepper
2 tablespoons vegetable oil
2 cups grated, raw potatoes
2 cups sauerkraut
2 cups apples, peeled, cored, diced to 1/4-inch cubes
1/4 cup white wine
2 tablespoons brown sugar
1/8 teaspoon caraway seed

In a large mixing bowl combine the meat, bread crumbs, egg, 1/2 cup of the onions, 1/2 teaspoon of the salt, stock, horseradish and pepper. Mix thoroughly. With wet hands form into tablespoon-sized meatballs. Brown the meatballs in the oil over medium heat. Roll to brown all sides.

While the meat is browning combine in another bowl the remaining ingredients — the potatoes, sauerkraut, apples, 1/4 cup onions, wine, brown sugar, 1/2 teaspoon salt and the caraway seed.

To assemble the dish, pour the second mixture into the bottom of a covered casserole dish. Arrange the meatballs on top. Bake in a preheated 350° oven for 1 hour.

The casserole will serve 4.

morning, noon and night. What I like, you'll like!" As he talked he raised a fist only slightly smaller than a hindquarter of moose. When it caught every eye in the room, he opened the fist in a sign of friendship. The fingers seemed the size of Polish sausages.

The troublemaker sat down and went back to eating his meatballs.

Meatball was quick to take advantage of his status. For breakfast the next morning he served sausage meatballs, eggs, pancakes and coffee. No one said a word.

During the next two weeks, however, the miners ate meatball dishes eight times. The meals were always good, but still there was muttering. Meatball was becoming a cussword in camp.

Then came payday. Meatball went to town on Saturday night and tripped off the wagon. He stayed in town drunk for a week. Cooked by others, the camp meals were awful, and the crew wanted him back, meatballs and all. They elected the troublemaker to go to town to find him.

He found Meatball and was driving him home when, coming down a mountain, he missed a curve. Their car plunged 160 feet before smashing on rock at the bottom of the cliff. Both men were killed outright.

After the funeral, a collection was taken to buy Meatball Johansen a grave marker, a simple marble slab with a pitted, basketball-sized sphere on the top. Maybe you've noticed it and thought it was a model of the moon to commemorate some astronaut buried there. Not so. It is John "Meatball" Johansen's grave. May he rest in peace. He successfully served meatballs to a mining crew five days in a row. No small accomplishment.

Perhaps you can match his success, using my recipes.

MEATBALLS HIPPIE

This one came to me marked "Bohemian" and caused considerable mental anguish. I had enough trouble with the term Bavarian, but this one created horrible visions of the hippies of the sixties and all the worst of that age. Then I was bothered because Bohemian food doesn't even have an ingredient such as caraway seed to establish its authenticity.

Remember the awful things the hippies did to our language? In spite of my hang-ups, I tried the recipe, man!

1 pound ground beef or moose
1/4 pound ground pork sausage
1/4 cup cracker crumbs
1 egg
2 tablespoons vegetable oil
1 15-ounce can tomatoes, broken
*   in pieces*
2 cups chopped onion
1 cup chopped green pepper
1/4 pound fresh mushrooms, or
*   1 4-ounce can mushrooms*
1 tablespoon chili powder
1 teaspoon salt
1/8 teaspoon pepper
1 cup cooked, drained macaroni

In a large mixing bowl combine beef, sausage, cracker crumbs and egg. Mix well. With wet hands form the meat into 1-inch balls. Brown them in oil over medium heat. Roll to brown all sides.

Add the tomatoes, onions, green pepper, mushrooms, chili powder, salt and pepper. Mix well and simmer for 30 minutes. Meanwhile cook the macaroni separately, drain it, and add it to the meat mixture during the last 10 minutes of cooking.

Go ahead, eat hippie. Set the skillet in the middle of the table. Add a big platter of bread. Oh, yes, and bowls.

VALDEZ PICADILLO

I first visited Valdez as a child in the summer of 1933. I last visited it in 1979, and it wasn't where I remembered it at all! The 1964 earthquake destroyed the old town, so the citizens just moved the site around the bay and built a modern little city.

This recipe has nothing to do with the town, unless folks there would like to adopt it. I first ate this dish while sitting on a cushion and drinking wine. (Wow! The naughty eighties!) I enjoyed the skilled guitar player who provided music too. So, have a party to serve this tasty dish.

1/4 cup beef stock, heated
1 cup golden seedless raisins
1 cup dark raisins
2 pounds lean ground beef or moose
2 tablespoons olive oil
2 cups dry red wine
3/4 cup finely chopped green onions
         with some tops
1-1/2 teaspoons salt
2 cloves garlic, minced fine
1/4 teaspoon oregano
1/4 teaspoon ground clove
1/4 teaspoon pepper
1 cup chopped green pepper
3/4 cup slivered almonds
3 cups cooked rice

Put the raisins to soak in the hot beef stock while you go on with the rest of the preparation.

In a large skillet over medium heat, add the oil and brown the meat, breaking it into small pieces as it cooks. When well browned, add the wine, onion, salt, garlic, oregano, clove and pepper. Simmer for 15 minutes.

Add the green pepper and stir while cooking another 5 minutes. Now add the raisins, stock and almonds and simmer until they are also hot.

Spoon mixture over a mound of hot cooked rice. Serve with a nice fresh salad and some hot hard rolls and a good wine. It serves 4 and maybe more.

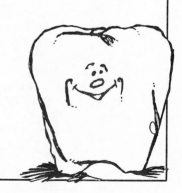

MATANUSKA MEATBALLS

Back when I found this recipe, the Matanuska Valley was producing both cottage cheese and Swiss chard, so I named the dish after the place. It takes some planning ahead, but it's worth the effort.

1-1/2 pounds lean ground beef
1 cup small curd cottage cheese
1/4 cup Parmesan cheese
1 cup finely chopped onion
1 egg
1 cup Swiss chard, only the green,
    chopped fine
1 teaspoon salt
1/4 teaspoon pepper
1/4 teaspoon garlic powder
1 cup beef stock
1 8-ounce can tomato sauce
1/4 cup dry white wine
2 tablespoons cornstarch

In a large bowl combine the meat, cheeses, onions, egg, chard and seasonings. Mix well with hands and, with wet hands, form into small meatballs. You should have 18 or so.

Place them in a well-greased baking pan and slide them into a preheated 450° oven for 30 minutes.

During that time combine the stock, tomato sauce and wine in a saucepan. Blend in the cornstarch. Cook over medium heat until the mixture thickens.

Remove the baking pan and reduce oven heat to 350°. Pour the stock mixture over the meatballs. Stir. Return the pan to the oven for another 30 minutes.

I would recommend serving these meatballs over rice, although the dish will stand by itself. It will make 4 people happy. Enjoy!

HONOLULU MEATBALLS
(Sweet-and-Sour)

Thanks to those men who named the section stations on The Alaska Railroad, I can say that I've passed Honolulu several times. The one day I visited Honolulu no one was at home. Still it makes an interesting name for a sweet-and-sour dish, don't you think? If you try it you can name it anything you wish, but try it.

1-1/2 slices dry bread, crust
    removed, diced
1/4 cup milk
1-1/2 pounds ground beef, moose or
    caribou
1 teaspoon salt
1/4 teaspoon pepper
1/2 cup finely minced onion
1 tablespoon dried parsley
1 12-ounce can jellied cranberry
    sauce
1 15-ounce can sauerkraut
1 12-ounce bottle chili sauce
2 tablespoons lemon juice

1 cup bread crumbs, rye or
    pumpernickel

In a large bowl soak the bread cubes in milk for a few minutes and then add the meat, salt, pepper, onion and parsley to the bowl. Mix thoroughly with the hands. With wet hands form teaspoon amounts into cocktail-size meatballs. Place them in a well-greased 13 x 9 x 2-inch baking pan. You should come up with 60 to 70 nice little meatballs.

In another pan combine the cranberry sauce, sauerkraut, chili sauce, lemon juice and bread crumbs. Over medium heat bring to a boil, reduce heat and simmer for 5 minutes, stirring often.

Pour the sauce over the meatballs so that all are covered. Place a piece of aluminum foil over the baking pan and slide it into a preheated 350° oven. Bake 45 minutes.

You can transfer the contents to a serving dish if you like, but I like to take the baking pan right to the table, or to a potluck dinner for many people to enjoy. It can easily be reheated.

I've never taken home anything from a potluck except an empty pan, but I never tell anyone there is sauerkraut in this recipe until after they have said they enjoyed it. A surprising number of people shy away from kraut without trying it.

ALASKAN CHICKEN PIE

My mother made chicken pot pie that I could have eaten three times a week. In fact, I hunted hard for the birds to go in her pies. Any game bird would do. I've changed her recipe in several ways, but mine still tastes good. Since it is a two-part recipe, read through before starting. But start soon.

2-1/2 cups cooked and boned
*   chicken, or 3 5-ounce cans of*
*   chicken, if you're in a hurry*
3 cups chicken stock
1/4 cup chopped celery
1 cup chopped onion
1 cup peeled and sliced carrots
1 bay leaf
2 tablespoons paprika
1/2 teaspoon salt
1/8 teaspoon pepper
1/4 cup butter or margarine
1/4 cup all-purpose flour

In a large saucepan combine the stock, celery, onions, carrots, bay leaf, paprika, salt and pepper. Bring to a boil and simmer 15 minutes. Remove from the heat and strain the vegetables from the liquid. Retain both. Discard bay leaf.

Melt butter in the pan and stir in the flour to make a roux. Return the liquid to the pan and cook over medium heat, stirring until gravy thickens.

Next spread the vegetables on the bottom of a 9 x 9-inch square baking pan and layer the chicken on top of the vegetables. Pour the thickened gravy over all and allow it to settle. Keep pan warm while you prepare the crust.

At this point you can reach for a stick of pie crust dough and proceed, as the package directs, to make a crust that will cover the baking pan.

Or you could pull out a box of biscuit mix and top the pie with biscuits.

If you feel lucky, bold or confident, try this unsual recipe "from scratch."

Sour Cream Pie Crust
1-1/2 cups all-purpose flour
1/2 teaspoon salt
2 teaspoons baking powder
1/2 teaspoon baking soda
2 eggs
3/4 cup sour cream
2 tablespoons milk

In a medium bowl sift flour, salt, baking powder and baking soda together.

In a separate bowl blend eggs and sour cream and stir them into the flour mixture. Mix well and pour onto the prepared chicken pie filling. Level, then brush the top with milk.

Bake in a preheated 425° oven for 20 minutes or until the top is nicely browned. The pie will serve 4.

PLAYING CHICKEN WITH REAL CHICKEN

CHAPTER
8

The word *chicken* can scarcely pass through my mind without reminding me of Timothy "Chicken" Randolph, an old man living in a cabin a quarter of a mile down the beach from us when I was a kid. He was a great admirer of my mother's cooking and was often at our dinner table on Sunday. He dearly loved chicken the way Mother fixed it.

I heard the story of Chicken Randolph many times during my youth. He had come to Alaska as a cabin boy aboard a full-rigged ship en route to Saint Michael on Norton Sound near the mouth of the Yukon River.

The ship had been overtaken by a wild storm while crossing the Gulf of Alaska. The skipper headed into Prince William Sound in search of shelter and a place to make some repairs.

Their ship, *Pride of the Northland*, touched an uncharted rock and began to fill. The deck cargo was several large boilers and steam engines destined for riverboats under construction. Knowing the ship would go down like a rock, the skipper ordered everyone to abandon ship.

Timothy and the ship's cook tried to launch the captain's gig, hanging in davits across the ship's stern. The gig reached the water, but the cook tangled in the lowering gear and was pulled out of the boat. The first sea swallowed him from sight.

That left young Timothy alone in the gig, except for five crates of chickens. They had been stored there as part of the ship's food supply. Timothy had twenty-five very wet and unhappy passengers in his first command.

Three days of drifting brought him in

sight of an island. Timothy rowed his gig ashore in a little cove. He pulled the craft up on the beach and unloaded the crates of chickens. One look at the miserable flock and he turned them loose to forage.

He found shelter in a cave for the night and woke to find his gig washed away by the tide. He was marooned.

He built a better shelter in the cave for himself and then for the chickens. He survived on small game and seafood. Before long the chickens learned to be survivors, too, and worked the beaches for sand fleas and bits of marine life.

By the first winter the flock had doubled in size. Timothy went into the hungry season with a few eating chickens available, although he planned to take only the extra roosters and maybe a few eggs.

By the next summer he witnessed a chicken catch and gulp down a small minnow. They were adapting to their new life as well as Timothy.

Five years passed before anyone found Timothy and his chickens. By then the chickens numbered over a thousand and overpopulation was becoming a problem. The man who found him, Ralph Timberline, had a solution to the problem. So the T&T Chicken Farm was formed. The

KALIFONSKY CHICKEN

The number of Russian place-names on the map of Alaska is good evidence that the Russians were here a while before they sold the land to the United States. Because so many recipes have come to me from towns with Russian names, I honor them with this dish:

2 whole chicken breasts, halved
1/2 cup white wine, the best you
    can afford
1/2 teaspoon thyme, crumbled
2 tablespoons vegetable oil
2 tablespoons butter or margarine
1/2 cup fresh bread crumbs
1/2 teaspoon salt
1/8 teaspoon pepper
1/4 cup Brazil nuts, slivered
1 cup seedless grapes (optional)

Combine wine and thyme in a bowl and marinate the chicken in this liquid for 4 hours, turning the pieces several times.

Heat oil in a heavy skillet over medium heat and add the butter. Combine bread crumbs, salt and pepper in a paper sack and shake the pieces of chicken in it. Then brown the chicken in the hot oil, turning once.

Place the chicken in a 13 x 9 x 2-inch baking pan and slide the pan into a preheated 350° oven. Bake for 15 minutes and remove. Sprinkle nuts and grapes over the chicken and return it to the oven for 5 minutes.

While the chicken is baking, stir the marinade into the skillet and cook over medium heat, scraping residue up from the bottom of the pan.

Remove the chicken to a serving plate and spoon the hot marinade over the chicken and fruit. Serves 4.

harvesting consisted of catching and butchering fifty chickens at a time. Ralph took the chicken meat to Seward, Valdez and Cordova.

Business boomed and they branched out to distribute fresh eggs the next year. The chickens did well and held their own in numbers. I remember Timothy telling about seeing a thousand white and red chickens marching out to the beach as the tide started out. The rim of birds followed the water as it receded.

Another year passed and suddenly there were cats on the island. Timothy imagined that a ship's cat had been washed overboard and made a long swim — a pregnant female cat, no doubt.

You can imagine how cats multiplied on an island full of chickens. When the issue of who was going to own the island became a war, Ralph brought Timothy a .22-caliber rifle to help even out the score.

As the quantity of chickens available for market continued to reduce, Ralph had a better idea. He began to butcher the cats being killed and to dress them like rabbits for frying. The T&T Chicken Farm had a

SALAMATOF CHICKEN

My mother-in-law fished the Salamatof Beach on Cook Inlet, northwest of Kenai, for many a season. The work was long and hard, but she found the time to provide good meals for her family, too.

This dish is good either hot or cold. You can take it fishing with you, and it'll be right at home.

12 pieces of chicken: 2 breasts
(halved), 4 thighs,
4 drumsticks
1 teaspoon salt
1/4 teaspoon pepper
1/4 teaspoon garlic powder
1-1/4 cups bread crumb
1/4 teaspoon mild chili powder
1/2 cup mustard (Dijon-style is best)
1/2 cup sour cream

Spread the chicken on a breadboard and sprinkle with salt, pepper and garlic powder. Combine bread crumbs and chili powder in a shallow dish. Mix well. Combine mustard and sour cream in another bowl and mix well. With a knife spread the mixture lightly over the chicken pieces. Roll the pieces in the bread crumbs and place in a 13 x 9 x 2-inch baking pan that has been lightly greased.

Bake in a preheated 400° oven for 45 minutes until chicken is tender and golden brown.

Serves 4 as a main meat course.

MURPHY'S FULL-DECK CHICKEN FRY

My friend Murphy, who is a terrific poker opponent — that is, one who loses much and constantly — is about as good with pots and pans as he is with playing cards, though he knows a good pizza if he sees one. When he invited me over for chicken dinner not long back, I assumed we'd be eating a store-bought one, for sure, prepared in some kitchen far away. Instead, he served me a dinner made from the following recipe, saying, "If *I* can do it, anyone can!" I was impressed, and you'd better believe I'm watching out for improvement in his cards, too.

2 frying chickens, cut into serving
    pieces (save the backs for
    stock)
1 quart vegetable oil
    (approximately)
1 12-ounce can flat beer
1-3/4 cups all-purpose flour
1-1/2 teaspoons salt
1/4 teaspoon pepper

Place your Dutch oven on high heat, pour in at least 1 inch of oil and heat it to 375°.

In a medium-sized bowl combine the beer, flour, salt and pepper. Beat with a wire whisk. Dip each piece of chicken in the batter until well coated. Let excess drip back into the bowl. Ease the pieces into the hot oil and allow them to cook 25 minutes,

turning once. If 2 batches are required, hold the first in a warm oven.

Murphy served 6 people that night, and if he can do it, so can you.

CHICKEN CURRY POLYNESIAN

When the family accepted the first dish I concocted that was heavy on curry flavor, I began to search for other recipes using the spice. Most I discovered were too exotic for my taste. One did come to light, finally, which didn't call for anything I couldn't find at the supermarket. I tried it. Why don't you?

4 whole chicken breasts, halved
1/2 cup butter or margarine
1/4 cup honey
1/4 cup ketchup
1 teaspoon salt
1/4 teaspoon garlic salt
1-1/2 cups pineapple juice, divided
1 tablespoon curry powder
1 tablespoon cornstarch
1 cup cherry tomatoes or
    Sweet 100's
1 green pepper, cut in chunks
1/2 cup salted cashews

I like to use the Dutch oven for this one. Heat butter in it over medium heat. Brown the chicken pieces, turning at least once. Now carefully drain as much fat as possible. Leave no more than a single tablespoonful in the pan.

In a bowl combine the honey, ketchup, salt, garlic salt and 1-1/4 cups of the pineapple juice. Add curry powder and stir well. Pour the liquid over the chicken pieces. Bring the mixture to a boil, lower heat, cover and simmer for 30 minutes.

Combine the remaining 1/4 cup pineapple juice with cornstarch and stir into pan juices until they thicken. Then add the tomatoes, green peppers and nuts. Cook uncovered for an additional 10 minutes, spooning the sauce over the chicken.

Serve over a mound of cooked rice. The dish will stand by itself, but a garnish is also nice. In a separate serving dish, offer a choice of chopped green onion, coconut shreds and — a favorite of mine — dried banana flakes. The dish will serve 6 people.

new product that was welcomed by the towns.

This enterprise prospered for nearly another year and then a disease came ashore and struck down the chickens. Inside a month they were gone. The cats soon were starving, although Ralph and Timothy marketed as many as possible.

Finally Timothy left the island and moved to Cordova but not before he and Ralph split a healthy bank account.

After hearing his story I always kept a close watch on my cat, Pudgie, though Timothy only once mentioned that Pudgie would make a good rabbit stew. And a nice pair of mittens. I hoped he was kidding me.

Our chickens of that time were often spruce hens or ptarmigan. It was part of my job to bring as many home as I could shoot. I can remember one New Year's Day I provided the dozen birds that Mother cooked. My older brother provided a venison roast. Dad dug the clams that made chowder for the first course. It was quite a dinner.

Later in life, as a trooper patrolling the highways, I became acquainted with another form of chicken — a game called "chicken." It consisted of two carloads of kids running head-on toward each other at a high rate of speed. The first one to recover his senses and turn away from the collision was the "Chicken!"

But I believe I will not tell you all the stories I know about that form of chicken. I am determined to put playing chicken back in the kitchen where it belongs. There it's a game I enjoy, too. Try some of these recipes to get in the action.

MR. PRESIDENT STEW

Since many of us are interested in the lives of famous people, their tastes in food are often exploited commercially. In Skagway, I ordered a "Soapy Smith Breakfast" and was served a bowl of oatmeal mush.

You can imagine how I approached a meal billed as "The President's Delight." But it turned out to be very good and I acquired the recipe for you.

3 pounds chicken thighs and
    drumsticks
1 teaspoon ground ginger
2 tablespoons vegetable oil
1 cup chopped onion
1 15-ounce can tomatoes
1 6-ounce can tomato paste
3 cloves garlic, minced
1/2 teaspoon cayenne
2-1/2 cups water, divided
1 cup creamy peanut butter
    (Now, guess which President!)
1 12-ounce package frozen okra
1 medium eggplant, peeled and cut
    in 1-inch cubes
1 chopped green pepper
1 sliced red pepper
4 hard-boiled eggs for garnish

Spread the chicken pieces on a breadboard and sprinkle with powdered ginger, rubbing it into both sides of the meat. Place the Dutch oven on medium heat and add the oil. Brown the chicken on all sides and remove to a side dish.

In the same oil, sauté the onions until transparent. Add tomatoes, tomato paste, garlic, cayenne and 2 cups of the water. Stir well and return the chicken to the pan. Bring to a boil and simmer for 30 minutes.

In a bowl combine the peanut butter with the remaining 1/2 cup water and stir into a smooth paste. Add the paste to the pot and stir. Add the okra, eggplant and peppers, red and green. Continue cooking for another 30 minutes, stirring occasionally.

Remove from heat, skim the fat, and season to taste with salt and pepper. Ladle the stew into a ring of hot rice. Garnish with egg quarters. The dish will serve 6 well.

MENTASTA CACCIATORE

By the banks of Mentasta Creek I ate a horrible meal the cook called "cacciatore." Silently, I ate his boiled spruce hen, all the while plotting to work out a better recipe and slip it to him. Here it is, Pete:

1 frying chicken, or several spruce
       hens, cut in serving pieces
1/4 cup vegetable oil or bacon
       grease
1 cup sliced onion
1 clove garlic, minced, or
       1/4 teaspoon garlic powder
1/4 cup chopped green pepper or
       1/8 cup dried pepper flakes
1/2 cup all-purpose flour
1 8-ounce can tomato sauce
1 teaspoon parsley
1/2 teaspoon oregano, crumbled
1/4 teaspoon thyme, crushed
1 teaspoon salt
1/2 cup water
1 4-ounce can mushroom stems
       and pieces (optional)

Heat oil in a Dutch oven and brown chicken on all sides. Remove meat and add onions, garlic and peppers and sauté until onions are tender. Add remaining ingredients, except mushrooms, and mix well. Return chicken to the pot, cover and cook over low heat 45 minutes, stirring occasionally. Add drained mushrooms during the last 10 minutes. Serves 4.

CORDOVA CHICKEN ROSEMARY

For the first twelve years of my life I didn't know Rosemary existed. Then she sat in front of me in school and I tormented her as boys will do. I was in love. I'm still in love with Rosemary, only . . . like this:

1 frying chicken, cut into serving
       pieces
3 tablespoons vegetable oil
1/2 cup chopped celery
1/2 cup chopped onion
1 clove garlic, minced
1 teaspoon salt
1/4 teaspoon pepper
1/4 teaspoon dried parsley
1-1/2 teaspoons rosemary, crushed
1/2 cup sherry

For this recipe reach for a large frying pan with a lid. Place it over medium heat, add the oil and brown the chicken pieces on all sides. Remove chicken and set aside.

To the same pan add celery, onion and garlic and sauté for 5 minutes. Stir in the salt, pepper, parsley and rosemary. Return the chicken to the pan. Stir to coat chicken with spices. Add sherry, cover and simmer until the chicken is done, about 30 minutes. During the last 10 minutes baste the chicken with the sauce.

Remove the chicken to a serving platter. Strain the cooking liquid and drizzle 1/4 cup of it over the chicken just before serving. Serves 4.

CHICKEN CHICKEN GINGER LEMON

Back in the summer of 1953 I chased a carload of would-be hard cases who were headed up the Taylor Highway toward the community of Chicken. When they ran out of gas a few miles to the south, they thought about having a gun battle with the chasing trooper. (Me, remember?) But after a quick look down the barrel of my riot gun, they chickened out. I was delighted.

Many hours later I managed to get home for dinner. Connie served me Chicken Ginger Lemon. I added a second chicken to the name in memory of that day.

3 whole chicken breasts, halved
*   and boned*
2 eggs
1 teaspoon sugar
1/2 teaspoon salt
1/8 teaspoon pepper
3 tablespoons vegetable oil
2 cloves garlic, sliced
3/4 cup nuts, cashews or
*   your choice*
1/3 cup cornstarch
1-1/2 cups Magie's Ginger Lemon
*   Sauce (see page 130)*

Place the chicken in a shallow pan. In a bowl beat the eggs and add sugar, salt and pepper. Pour the egg mixture over the chicken and turn pieces to coat. Set aside.

Heat the vegetable oil in a large skillet over medium heat. Sauté the garlic and brown the nuts for a few minutes. Remove the solids from the skillet. Reserve the nuts. Put the cornstarch in a paper sack and shake each piece of chicken to coat with the cornstarch. Place the chicken pieces in the skillet and cook over low heat until both sides are browned. Five minutes per side is about right.

Transfer the chicken pieces to a

94   PLAYING CHICKEN

13 x 9 x 2-inch baking pan. Add Magie's Ginger Lemon Sauce to the skillet and stir around to pick up the browning residue as you bring the liquid to a boil. Pour the hot sauce over the chicken.

Bake at 350° for 30 minutes. Sprinkle the nuts on the top and bake another 5 minutes. Remove to a platter for serving. The dish will please 6 if there are plenty of accompanying foods like potatoes, vegetables and a salad.

NELSONI ORIENTAL CHICKEN

Way back in my youth, when I was serving as helper to a Chinese cook aboard a cannery tender, I watched him spread a mysterious special sauce over chicken pieces and then slide them into the oven. The chicken was delicious, but only recently did I discover what the sauce really was. Are you ready for this? It was only orange marmalade, prepared this way:

2 tablespoons butter
1 large onion, minced
1/4 cup orange marmalade
1 frying chicken, cut in serving
    pieces
Salt and pepper

In a small frying pan melt the butter and sauté the onion until it is transparent. Add marmalade, take pan off the heat and stir.

Place chicken pieces in a 13 x 9 x 2-inch baking pan that has been lightly greased. Sprinkle with salt and pepper. Spoon a small amount of marmalade sauce onto each piece. Spread the remaining sauce on the larger pieces.

Bake in a preheated 325° oven for 1 hour or until the chicken is tender. Serves 4.

DRY CREEK CASSEROLE CREOLE

Way back during World War II, the U.S. Army had a camp at Dry Creek near the Gulkana Airport. It was designed as a place to fall back to in case the Japanese took Anchorage.

At this camp I found an imaginative mess sergeant, one of the army's rarest individuals. The meat in his dish was pork, but not the Spam that was so common in army cooking. Instead he used pork sausage patties from C-rations, all nicely cubed. It was a good recipe I've modified slightly.

1 pound cooked pork, cubed small
    (or sausage or Spam)
2 cups chopped onion
1 cup cooked elbow macaroni
1 15-ounce can tomatoes
1 cup shredded Cheddar cheese
1 teaspoon salt
1/4 teaspoon cinnamon
1/2 cup bread crumbs

In a large skillet over medium heat, brown the meat and sauté the onions. Drain fat from the skillet and add remaining ingredients except bread crumbs. Mix well and pour into a casserole dish. Sprinkle bread crumbs on top.

Slide into a preheated 325° oven for 45 minutes. The casserole will serve 4.

MENDELTNA CURRY CASSEROLE

One night in 1953 I was on my way home from one of those eighteen-hour days that seemed the rule rather than the exception for an outpost trooper. I turned into Mendeltna Lodge in search of a hamburger to sustain life until I could reach home. The place was empty except for one of the owners. She was just sitting down to dinner and said no to my request for a hamburger. Instead she waved me into the chair opposite her and slid a plate across to me.

Then she lifted the cover from a wonderful smelling casserole in the middle of the table and dished me a helping. Wow! You *must* taste it to believe how good it was:

2 cups cooked pork, cut in 1/2-inch
    cubes
3 cups cooked brown rice
1 15-ounce can peas, drained
1 15-ounce can sliced carrots,
    drained
1/2 teaspoon salt (less if pork
    already salted)
1/8 teaspoon pepper
1-1/2 cups Curry Casserole Sauce
    (see page 133)

Combine all ingredients in a casserole with a cover. Mix well and slide into a preheated 350° oven for 30 minutes or until the dish is as hot as you desire. Yield: 4 servings.

FINGER-LICKING RIBS TO SPARE

CHAPTER 9

Living in Alaska for the first few years of my life, I thought the only meats provided by a pig were bacon and sowbelly or, as the latter is known, salt pork. The first fried up crisp and delicious. The second was an old friend that made beans taste good.

Then one day ham made its appearance in my life and I became a fan of the wonderful meat. We weren't told that it wasn't good to eat because it had been preserved with dangerous substances such as salt, smoke and nitrates. (Or is it nitrites?) Heck, we didn't even have a name for cancer yet. Back in those days ham didn't kill you through food poisoning, either.

And we *were* careless about preserved meats. I can remember chunks of slab bacon lying unrefrigerated for days. Who had refrigerators?

Bacon rind was a useful and versatile item. A small piece was nice for greasing a frying pan. My older brother, however, managed to bring home the limping family boat, *Pep,* one time by lining the marine clutch with a section of bacon rind. Another time, the bearing on a dock-yard hoisting engine was "temporarily" replaced with a bacon rind that was still serving that useful function when we left town years later.

I even patched the bottom of a skiff with a chunk of bacon rind. I battered the broken board back in place, covered it with bacon rind and nailed another board on top. We didn't get around to making a real patch until the following summer.

MABLE'S HASH

Almost as soon as my first cookbook reached the public, I began receiving letters and recipes, most of them someone's favorite. One that came out tasting of kerosene puzzled me. But, Mable, yours was definitely a winner. Let's share it with many?

2 cups cooked pork, cubed small
    (ham works, too)
2 cups cooked, minced sweet
    potatoes (canned okay)
1/4 cup juice from canned
    pineapple slices
1/4 teaspoon prepared mustard
4 slices canned pineapple
2 tablespoons brown sugar
1 tablespoon butter or margarine

Combine the pork, sweet potatoes, pineapple juice and mustard in a bowl. Pour the mixture evenly into a greased or nonstick casserole or oven-safe skillet. Lay the slices of pineapple on top. Sprinkle on the sugar and dot with butter.

Bake in a preheated 350° oven for 30 minutes. Remove and take the casserole straight to the table. It will serve 4. Thanks, Mable!

Sowbelly, when it wasn't going into the bean pot, often found its way into boiled dinners and cabbage dishes. Sometimes I tied small cubes of it to mousetraps. The field mice moving into our house for the winter couldn't leave the stuff alone.

Even today, whenever I see salt pork in a market, I invariably find a chunk of it in my grocery sack when I get home, though I'm the only member of the family really fond of it.

I was in my teens before pork chops entered my life, followed shortly by pork roasts. But the most outstanding pork discovery of my life was spareribs. The first I tasted were simply oven baked, crispy and fantastic!

Then someone from the second biggest state in the Union visited us and gave us barbecuing. Shorty was that Texan's name. He thought nothing was fit to eat without barbecue sauce on it. At breakfast he painted his fried eggs with the sauce and his steak at the evening meal. He did not make full converts of us, but we did love Shorty's barbecued ribs.

As civilization crept into Alaska, pork became a common meat almost everywhere I wandered. It faded from the menus farther north where other fatty foods such as muktuk and seal oil were available.

The biggest pork chop I ever ate was served me at the roadhouse at Bethel. Since the dinner was served family style, I reached out and forked a chunk of meat as big as my dinner plate. And you can bet I had another when the platter came around the second time.

After all it was 50° below zero outside, and the wind had the chill factor up around 100° below. In that kind of weather you need fuel to survive.

In the morning I made an end run back to Anchorage, where it was a warm 10° below and windless. It seemed balmy as I stepped off the plane.

GUSTAVUS PORK

One day when we were on a search effort a few miles west of Juneau near Glacier Bay, a storm put us down at the Gustavus airstrip. As usual in such cases, wonderful townspeople gave us dinner and a place to throw down our sleeping bags. Luckily, we'd picked roast pork night and were served:

1 boneless pork roast, about
    3 pounds
1/4 cup vegetable oil
1 clove garlic, minced
1 No. 2½ can (1 lb. 13 oz.)
    sauerkraut
6 medium potatoes
Salt and pepper to taste

Put the oil and garlic in a Dutch oven over medium heat. Season the pork with salt and pepper and brown all sides in the hot oil.

While the meat is browning, open a can of sauerkraut and drain well, saving the liquid.

Remove browned meat, pour off the juices and save. Line the bottom of the pot with the drained sauerkraut. Place the meat on top. Return the browning juices to the meat and add 2 tablespoonfuls of kraut juice to the pot.

Cover the Dutch oven and slide it into a preheated 325° oven for 1 hour. Then lift the lid and place the potatoes around the meat. Return to oven for about 70 minutes more.

Serves 6 people, even hungry ones.

KENAI PORK

Pork roasts I used to cook were always dry, as if I'd burned the pen down around the pig. Then one day, somebody down in the Kenai area served me pork roast barbecued in the oven. It was so easy, I wondered why I hadn't figured out how to do it on my own.

1 pork roast, 4 pounds or more
2 tablespoons vegetable oil
1 bottle commercial barbecue
    sauce, or try Blodgett
    Barbecue Sauce (see
    page 124)
Salt, pepper to taste

Add the oil to your Dutch oven and place it over medium heat. Brown the roast on all sides. Pour barbecue sauce over the meat, cover the Dutch oven and slide it into a preheated 325° oven for 1 hour.

Slide from the oven, open the pan and baste the meat. Return it, uncovered, to oven for another 30 minutes. Baste again and return for a last 15 minutes.

I usually bake potatoes to accompany the roast. A 4-pound roast will serve 6.

SEWARD SAUSAGE PIE

The city of Seward is fast becoming one of the country's leading seafood packagers. An invitation to dinner there left me with my mouth all set for seafood. What I was served wasn't seafood, but it was so good I must share it with you.

1-1/2 pounds ground pork sausage
2 eggs, beaten
2-1/2 cups cooked, mashed sweet
*   potatoes*
3/4 cup orange juice
1 teaspoon grated orange peel
1/2 teaspoon salt
1/4 teaspoon nutmeg

In a skillet over medium heat fry the sausage, breaking up the larger pieces, until browned. Drain and spread on the bottom of 9-inch pie pan.

In a bowl combine the beaten eggs, sweet potatoes, orange juice, orange rind, salt and nutmeg. Mix well and spread on top of the meat. Level and smooth.

Slide into a preheated 375° oven for 30 minutes. Remove from oven, cool for 10 minutes. Then invert the pie onto a serving plate. Cut into pie-shaped pieces and serve to 6.

A **few days ago** I attended a stand-up-and-hope-to-find-a-place-to-sit-down dinner where the sideboard offered a surprising assortment of good things to eat. A fine boneless ham caught my eye. My first bite brought back memories of Ben's smokehouse bear and I went back for seconds to honor the memory of Ben's ham. I also filled my glass at the bar in honor of Jack Daniels.

Sometime later I cornered my host to ask about the ham. His recipe was new and exciting to a ham lover. He had purchased a boneless ham of some ten pounds at the local supermarket; you know, the ordinary type that says, "water added." He unwrapped it from all its covering and placed it on the top rack of his little smoker and kept hickory smoke surrounding it for eight to ten hours. I've tried it, and the process results in near-authentic country-cured flavor.

But enough of whetting the appetite. Let's get on with the meal.

LEONA'S PORK CHOP SURPRISE

Leona was my mother's name, although she was always called Toni. Here is one of her recipes that I have altered some to include ingredients available today.

4 lean pork chops
1 tablespoon vegetable oil
1/4 can cream of mushroom soup
   (or an equal amount of thick
   white sauce)
1/4 cup milk
1/4 cup creamy peanut butter
1 teaspoon Worcestershire
1 teaspoon salt
1/8 teaspoon pepper
4 onion slices, 1/4 inch thick

In a skillet with a cover, heat the oil over medium heat. Brown the pork chops on both sides. Drain the fat from the skillet.

In a bowl combine the soup, milk, peanut butter, Worcestershire, salt and pepper. Place an onion slice on each chop and pour liquid over the meat.

Simmer, covered, for 45 minutes.

Serve with boiled potatoes so as not to waste any of the excellent gravy. Serves 2 to 4.

TROOPER PORK CHOPS

I have in my files some fifty different ways to cook pork chops. This recipe was dreamed up by a man I helped in line of duty. Since I wouldn't let him name it after me, he settled on "Trooper."

6 pork loin chops
Salt and pepper
1 tablespoon vegetable oil
2 tablespoons cornstarch
1/4 teaspoon garlic salt
1/2 teaspoon rosemary, crushed
1/2 cup water
2 tablespoons lemon juice
6 lemon slices

Spread the chops out on a breadboard and season with salt and pepper. Add the oil to a skillet with a cover and brown the chops over medium heat, turning once. Remove to another dish.

Add the cornstarch, garlic salt, rosemary and 1/2 cup water to the skillet. Return to low heat and stir constantly to prevent lumps from forming. Cook until the liquid is thick and glossy. Now add the lemon juice.

Return the chops to the pan, add a lemon slice to each, cover and simmer for 50 minutes.

This dish might serve 6, but plan on serving only 3 who are pork chop eaters.

LUAU
SUCKLING
PIG

I have always loved a good party and the luau has long been one of my favorites. I guess I like grass skirts, legs and all those good things. During our time in Juneau we threw several, sometimes serving fish, once spareribs and a few odd pineapples. Thinking big, however, I dreamed of cooking a whole pig — if not a 500-pound pig, at least a suckling pig of up to 20 pounds. I studied how to go about it and fulfilled my fantasy. In case you've been harboring a like ambition, here's how I did it:

1 suckling pig, 15 to 25 pounds,
    dressed, but with tail, head
    and feet intact, eyes removed
1/2 cup butter
2 loaves dry bread, diced (dressing
    mix okay)
2 cups chopped onion
2 teaspoons salt
1/2 teaspoon pepper
1/4 teaspoon cinnamon
2 cups chicken stock
1 red apple
2 maraschino cherries

You will need to buy or borrow a large roasting pan. It should be big enough to hold the pig and small enough to fit in your oven. Once this hurdle is passed, you can wash the pig inside and out and dry it carefully.

In a large mixing bowl combine the melted butter, bread cubes, onion, salt, pepper, cinnamon and chicken stock. Mix well and stuff the pig's cavity loosely with the dressing. Sew up the opening.

Place a wooden block in the pig's mouth so it will remain open to receive the apple later. Cover the pig's ears and cute little tail with foil to protect from burning. Place the pig in the roasting pan, right side up, with the legs neatly tucked under to form a rack to hold the pig upright.

Roast the pig in a 325° oven for 6 or 7 hours. If it browns too quickly, protect the back from burning with an aluminum foil tent.

When the pig is done, carefully transfer it to a large serving platter. I used a breadboard covered with aluminum foil. Allow to cool for 15 minutes. Remove the wooden block and insert the red apple into the mouth. The cherries go in the eye sockets.

Now, you will likely not do this very often, so go all the way. Add a lei of flowers around the pig's neck and be sure to make a production of serving the roast.

It will serve up to 15 people.

I am available for parties like this. No, not to cook! To be a guest.

SPARERIBS TO TRAVEL

I dearly love spareribs cooked in many ways. All my family loves ribs and many of my friends love ribs. My recipe file runneth over with recipe ideas. Here is the best:

*1 rack pork spareribs, cut into
    serving pieces*
*1 batch Blodgett Barbecue Sauce
    (see page 124)*
Salt, pepper, garlic salt, celery salt

Spread the rib pieces out on a breadboard and season with salt, pepper, garlic salt and celery salt to your taste.

Arrange the pieces on a rack in a 13 x 9 x 2-inch baking pan. Add hot water to the pan to just below the rack. Do not let the water reach the ribs.

Slide the baking pan into a preheated 450° oven and cook for 20 minutes. Slide the pan out, turn the ribs over and add water as needed. Reduce the heat to 300° and cook another 30 minutes.

Slide the pan out and paint the ribs with barbecue sauce on both sides. Return to the oven for 20 minutes more.

If you want to serve the ribs now, remove them from the pan, paint them again with barbecue sauce and place them on a platter. Serve with extra sauce in a pitcher and lots of paper napkins. They'll feed 4 people.

But if you want to serve them later, at a picnic, for instance, let them cool, paint them again with sauce and wrap in foil. Refrigerate until needed.

When it's time to eat the ribs, remove the foil, paint the ribs with barbecue sauce again, and slide them under a broiler about 3 inches from the heat source for 5 to 10 minutes. Watch carefully so as not to burn this wonderful meat. Adjust distance and heat as necessary.

Cooking ribs can be dangerous. Anytime you have opened the oven door to check the ribs, step back cautiously. There is bound to be someone standing right behind you. That barbecue smell always draws a crowd.

CORDOVA BANANA SALAD

I've had a love affair with the banana ever since I traded half a bean sandwich for my first one. That was in Cordova, and the year was 1931.

Naturally the idea of banana salad fascinated me and I enjoyed this recipe when it was sent me. It's just enough to serve one person.

2 ripe bananas
2 tablespoons finely chopped nuts, peanuts, pecans, or what you have
1 tablespoon mayonnaise
1 leaf lettuce

Peel and slice the banana into nice thin slices. Mix in a bowl with the nuts. Add mayonniase and stir to coat everything. Turn out on a lettuce leaf, on a salad plate, and serve.

This salad should be made as near eating time as possible since cut bananas darken if left standing. If you wish to increase the recipe to serve several people and want to make the salad a short time ahead, sprinkle the banana slices with lemon juice before you add nuts and mayonnaise. Taste and add a bit of sugar if it's needed. Leave the salad in the mixing bowl until serving time.

IMAGINATION BEAN SALAD

Over the years I have discovered many people living in Alaska's Bush who are imaginative both in and out of their kitchens. This recipe is from a woman who rates a "10" on all counts.

1 15-ounce can pork and beans in tomato sauce
1 tablespoon soy sauce
1/4 teaspoon ground ginger
1/8 teaspoon garlic salt
1/4 cup green onions, sliced thin
1/4 cup celery, cut in thin, diagonal slices
2 tablespoons chopped green pepper or dried pepper flakes, plumped in a small amount of water
1 8-ounce can pear halves, drained and cubed

In a medium-sized bowl combine the beans, soy sauce, ginger and garlic salt. Mix well and add onions, celery, green pepper and mix again. Then fold in the pear cubes and chill at least 2 hours. Serve in individual bowls. Serves 4.

UP SHIP CREEK WITH A SALAD

CHAPTER
10

To many of us old Alaskans, the creek that separates the military bases, Elmendorf Air Force Base and Fort Richardson, from Anchorage brings back memories. The creek, named Ship Creek, flows into Cook Inlet. Incidentally, the proper spelling is *S-H-I-P*, though people from the Lower 48 seem to question that. Many call it by a name that has a "T" in it. (Isn't "THIP" a helluva' funny name? Maybe they all lisp.) But enough of that. I've got a story to tell.

When World War II was just nicely getting started, I entered the U.S. Army. On July 3, 1942, I was sworn in and shipped out within the hour — overseas. That is, I took a truck ride across Ship Creek to Fort Richardson.

We were off-loaded at the 4th Infantry training camp where we dumped our gear in the Quonset huts and immediately walked to lunch. (We were not into marching yet.)

The moment I entered the mess hall, I saw the biggest salad I have ever seen. There, in a 2 by 3-foot food service tray and piled another foot above its 8-inch sides, was potato salad.

As I walked past the serving station, a large glob of the salad was splatted into my tray. I wasn't frightened, then, but the S.O.S.* at the next station was terrifying.

Since the color of the potato salad was not familiar, I examined its contents. It had been made of scrambled, powdered eggs in place of boiled eggs. The mess sergeant had done the impossible. He made

*If you don't know this dish, ask a close friend who's been in the service to translate for you.

powdered eggs taste good. Two days later he was transferred to the Officer's Club.

Once the restrictions of basic training were over and I was assigned to a unit, I discovered passes, my chance to escape back "overseas" to Anchorage. I began to make salads on my own again, and even better, to encourage members of the opposite sex, who felt an obligation to entertain members of the armed forces, to cook for me, among other things.

As this is a cookbook, however, and not an exposé, I will confine myself to a story from a later period of my life that illustrates the most generally accepted method for "finding one's way to a man's heart," that is, through his stomach.

One of my longtime Anchorage friends, developed during those days of army service, was a fellow named Art, a most eligible bachelor who *wanted* to be married. His handicap: he was terrified of females, all females, but particularly those who were like him, unmarried.

I took him aside and explained in some detail that girls were people, too. They had the same feelings, likes and dislikes he did. Many of them even wanted to get married. I suggested that he run around with a smile on his face and talk to women. Instead, my wise counsel produced a silly grin and a tongue-tied and solemn boy. I gave up on him.

Then to the community came Ellen Mae, an attractive, friendly, outgoing person. She met Art at our house one evening. I would like to report that they left together, but no way.

Next day, Art told me he liked Ellen Mae, although the only words he had spoken to her were, "Glad to know you!"

Meanwhile back at home, Ellen Mae was telling Connie that she was attracted to Art. This sparked Connie's matchmaking efforts, and I found myself feeding two extra people about three times a week while the plot bubbled.

Eventually the girls' efforts culminated in the Great Fruit Salad Ploy. To one meal, Ellen Mae brought an enormous bowl of fruit salad mingled with a rich whipped-cream dressing and topped with cherries. Art consumed at least half of it while he babbled compliments to Ellen Mae with every other bite. That evening, finally, he became brave enough to walk her home. Bingo!

BUSH SHOESTRING SALAD

In the middle of an Alaskan winter, the price of lettuce, tomatoes and cukes climbs very high. In fact, these vegetables develop much in common with gold. Having neither the fresh stuff nor the gold, imaginative cooks in Bush country have to look for other ingredients. From a cook "out there" comes this recipe.

1 cup cooked chicken, boned and
*   cut in chunks, or try tuna*
1 cup shredded carrots
1 cup sliced celery (if available!)
1/4 cup minced onion
1/2 cup Miracle Whip
*   salad dressing*
1 tablespoon cream or undiluted
*   evaporated milk*
1 teaspoon vinegar
1/2 teaspoon sugar
1 5-ounce can shoestring potatoes
*   or chow mein noodles*

Combine the chicken, carrots, celery and onion in a large bowl. In another bowl combine the salad dressing, cream, vinegar and sugar. Pour the dressing over the vegetables and let stand until just before serving.

At the last minute add the shoestring potatoes and lightly mix. Serves 4 to 6.

Art didn't report for work the next morning. Concerned, I stopped by his cabin on my way home in the afternoon. He said he was down with the flu or something. Privately I figured he had OD'd on fruit salad.

I mentioned this to Connie when I reached home. She at once called Ellen Mae. In a flash she whipped up another fruit salad, complete with cherries, and swooped down on Art like an angel of mercy, bringing the sustenance of life and brimming with sympathy. I don't know, nor did I want to know, how long she stayed that evening.

One week later I was best man at their wedding. Connie was matron of honor.

Even today I can get a rise out of Art by mentioning fruit salad and its mysterious powers. When their kids get a little older somebody should explain it to them. The susceptibility to it may run in the family.

Though fruit wasn't the route to my marriage, I, too, have been a salad lover since the days I cranked the handle of the food chopper while Mother made coleslaw, and I looked forward to licking the mixing bowl when she turned the salad out into a serving dish.

My travels back and forth in Alaska for fifty years and more have allowed me to eat in a hundred places serving food to the public and in a lot of private homes. I have found our people imaginative in preparing salads.

Oddly, the least appealing salads often were served in the areas with the greatest access to good produce . . . as in a restaurant I visited recently in one of Alaska's larger cities. The salad, accompanying a meal that cost fifteen dollars a head, consisted of a few shreds of lettuce, a couple shreds of red cabbage, half a radish and a micromillimeter thin slice of pale tomato doused with a watery oil and vinegar dressing. Sound familiar?

Back to the imaginative salads. I'm delighted to share some with you in this chapter because, though nothing can replace meat and potatoes or pasta for me, I am a firm believer that salads are an important part of most any meal and, as such, should be prepared with respect and well served.

THINK LOBSTER SALAD

A number of years ago I attended a party at the home of a couple who had too much money. There I tasted lobster salad and had the stray thought that I could get used to eating this salad. Since I couldn't afford to I created the Think Lobster Salad. You eat halibut, thinking lobster. It works!

1 pound halibut
1 celery top
1-1/4 teaspoons salt, divided
2 tablespoons lemon juice
1 head lettuce, separated into
    leaves
1-1/2 cups sliced celery
1/4 cup diced green pepper
1/2 teaspoon thyme, crumbled
1/8 teaspoon pepper
1/4 cup mayonnaise
8 radishes, cut into flowers

Prepare the fish sometime before you plan to assemble the salad as the fish must be cold. Tie the fish and the celery top in a cheesecloth bag and place in boiling water to which a teaspoon of salt has been added. Cook gently for 15 minutes, until the fish flakes easily but is not overcooked. Remove the fish from the bag and spread on a plate. Sprinkle the fish with the lemon juice and chill.

When it's time to assemble the salad, arrange lettuce leaves on individual salad plates.

Carefully remove any skin and fat from the halibut and flake the meat.

Combine the celery, green pepper, thyme, remaining 1/4 teaspoon salt, pepper and mayonnaise. Mix well, gently adding in the fish.

Divide fish mixture between individual salad plates. Sprinkle with paprika and decorate with radish flowers. Think lobster and enjoy! (Simply smile appreciatively if a guest believes it's real lobster!)

Yield: 4 to 6 servings.

SHANGHAI CHOY SALAD

This recipe was given me by a little old lady who claimed to have been born in China but would never supply the date of her birth. She talked at great length about growing up there and how she had hated to leave when her parents returned to the United States.

She wished to go back, but by the time China began accepting American visitors, she was no longer with us. I have only the recipe to remember her.

2 cups cooked ham, diced
1/4 cup French dressing
1 tablespoon soy sauce
1 16-ounce can bean sprouts,
    drained well, or about 2 cups
    fresh bean sprouts
1/4 cup chopped onion
1/2 cup thinly sliced sweet pickle
1/4 teaspoon salt
3/4 cup mayonnaise
Pepper
Lettuce

In a shallow bowl, marinate the ham in a mixture of French dressing and soy sauce. Marinate under refrigeration 30 minutes to 1 hour.

Add the drained or fresh bean sprouts, onions, pickle, salt and mayonnaise and mix well. Pepper to taste. Turn out onto salad plates lined with lettuce. Serves 6.

LOUIE'S CRAB SALAD

Our family has been adding crab meat to salads for fifty years, but since we moved away from our crab traps out in the bay, the expensive critter has almost disappeared from our diet.

Still, no matter what its price per pound, it's cheaper than maintaining a boat. When I weaken and actually purchase crab, it most always goes right into a delicious salad.

1 medium head lettuce
1/2 teaspoon salt
1 pound crab meat, any variety
1 cucumber, peeled and sliced
4 tomatoes, sliced
3 hard-boiled eggs, sliced
1 cup mayonnaise
1 tablespoon lemon juice
1 tablespoon chopped sweet pickle

In the bottom of a good-sized bowl, spread washed and well-dried lettuce leaves. Sprinkle with salt. Arrange the crab meat over the lettuce. Arrange the cucumber, tomatoes and egg slices over the crab.

In a smaller bowl combine mayonnaise, lemon juice and pickle. Pour the dressing over the salad. It serves 4 to 6 people.

(Louie? He's the guy who sold me the crab!)

ROADHOUSE SALAD

Back in the early days of Alaska, stage coaches and dog teams were the way to travel. Since they seldom made more than twenty miles a day, roadhouses sprang up about that far apart along the well-traveled routes. These places served plain but plentiful meals for the most part.

As always there were cooks who tried a little harder because of personal pride. Serving a good salad in the wintertime was a special challenge. Though coleslaw and potato salad were standbys, here's how one imaginative roadhouse cook turned familiar ingredients into something special.

3 cups cooked beets, peeled and diced small
3 cups cooked potatoes, peeled and diced
1 cup raw apples, peeled, diced
3 pickles, gherkins, or what's available, diced
4 hard-cooked eggs, chopped
1/4 cup mayonnaise or more if needed
Salt and pepper

In a bowl combine the beets, potatoes, apples and pickles and mix lightly. Add the eggs and mix again. Add the mayonnaise and turn carefully until everything is coated. Salt and pepper to taste. Serves 4 to 6.

PALMER CALICO SALAD

In the Matanuska Valley, on the outskirts of Palmer, is the Alaska State Fairgrounds. Here, for ten days in the fall, we have fun and games. As at state fairs anywhere, the things produced on local farms are in the spotlight. In Palmer, cabbage is king. Even a fifty-pound one isn't in the running for a blue ribbon. I've seen sixty- and seventy-pound cabbages — great fun to look at but I always think, "What in the world is a cook to do with that much cabbage?!"

I'll take the smaller ones, in assorted colors, please. Here's an assorted-color salad of my mother's which I've renamed to honor the fair.

1-1/2 cups shredded red cabbage
1-1/2 cups shredded green cabbage
1/4 cup minced onion
1/2 cup Miracle Whip salad dressing
1 tablespoon vinegar
2 tablespoons sugar
1/4 teaspoon salt
1/4 teaspoon celery salt

In a large bowl combine the cabbages and onion. In a smaller bowl, whip together the salad dressing, vinegar, sugar, salt and celery salt.

Pour the dressing over the cabbage and mix well. Serves 4.

FREEZEUP SALAD

In the fall that worst of all days arrives — the first hard freeze that will kill all the goodies in the garden. Since I can't let that happen without a fight, I pick as many vegetables as I can ahead of time for salads. One like this uses quite a number.

3 carrots, thinly sliced
3 zucchini, 6 to 8 inches long, sliced
    thinly
4 green onions, chopped well into
    the green
1/2 cup vegetable oil
2 tablespoons lemon juice
1/2 teaspoon salt
1/4 teaspoon pepper
1 teaspoon curry powder

In a medium bowl combine the carrots, zucchini and onions. In a smaller bowl whip together the oil, lemon juice, salt, pepper and curry powder. Pour the dressing over the vegetables and toss to coat. Chill for at least 2 hours before serving.

To save even more goodies from freezeup (and make a still tastier salad) add some of the following:

8 broccoli flowerettes
8 cauliflower flowerettes
8 Sugar Snap peas, pod and all

Get the idea?

DEEP WINTER SALAD

As I sit here typing, I can read the temperature on the thermometer outside — 30° below zero. I don't know the chill factor, but I can hear the wind whipping around the house. The driveway is full of drifts. I am not going to the store today, certainly; maybe not this week. I'll just look around the cupboard for the makings of a nice, hot salad.

*2 6-1/2-ounce cans tuna, drained of
    oil or water*
2 cups chopped celery
1/2 cup minced onion
1 cup Miracle Whip salad dressing
2 tablespoons lemon juice
1/2 cup slivered almonds
1/4 teaspoon salt
*2 cups toast cubes (toast bread on
    both sides, butter and cube it)*

In a large bowl combine the tuna, celery, onion, salad dressing, lemon juice, almonds, salt and 1 cup of the toast cubes. Mix these well and divide between 4 well-greased ramekins. Distribute remaining toast cubes on top.

Slide into a preheated 450° oven for 15 minutes. Remove ramekins to plates and serve at once.

Yield: 4 servings.

GOTTA' TRY SALAD

When I find or receive a recipe that I think is promising, I toss it into the basket marked, "Gotta' Try!"

I was about to close out this section on salads when a recipe fell out of that basket. *You* gotta' try it!

1/4 cup mayonnaise
2 tablespoons soy sauce
*1 clove garlic, crushed (or 1/4
    teaspoon garlic powder)*
1/4 teaspoon sugar
*3 cups shredded romaine, or try
    cabbage*
*1 16-ounce can bean sprouts,
    drained, or about 2 cups fresh*
8 radishes, sliced thin
4 green onions, sliced thin

In a large bowl beat together the mayonnaise, soy sauce, garlic and sugar. Add the lettuce, sprouts, radishes and onions. Toss lightly to coat everything. Serve at once to 4.

With an addition or two, and slightly more dressing, this salad can become the main dish for lunch. Try adding a small, well-drained can of chunk tuna, chicken, shrimp, salmon or crab (if you're rich). Or a cup or so of cold meat chunks or cheese cubes.

KNIK CREAM OF ONION SOUP

When I was wandering the Knik River area one day, I found Maude and her famous cream of onion soup. We talked, tasted her soup, and I collected a new recipe. Then her husband came home and I served a summons on him. At first he was angry, but then he saw the humor in the situation. We had another bowl of the soup together and I escaped with only a good recipe.

1/4 cup butter
1 cup finely sliced onion
1/2 teaspoon curry powder
3 tablespoons flour
2 cups beef stock (or 4 bouillon
  cubes and 2 cups water)
2 cups milk
Salt and pepper
Croutons

In a saucepan melt the butter and sauté the onions over medium heat. When they are just transparent, add the curry powder and stir to coat the onions well.

Add the flour, blend, then the stock, and stir constantly until the liquid thickens. Add the milk and continue to cook — without letting the liquid boil — until the onions are tender. You can add more milk if desired.

Serve in deep bowls with croutons on top, or I like to add Spoon Size Shredded Wheat biscuits, instead.

WIGGLING FISH SOUP

During the fishing season I freeze as much fish for later as I can. But fresh fish remains my favorite. A soup made with fish so fresh that it's still quivering, if not wiggling, is the best.

I would suggest you prepare some of this recipe ahead so the fresh-caught fish can go right to the pot with as little time loss as possible.

1 tablespoon vegetable oil
1 cup chopped onion
1-1/2 cups chicken stock
1 6-ounce can tomato paste
1 teaspoon minced fresh ginger
  or 1/2 teaspoon powdered
1 teaspoon curry powder
1/4 teaspoon cayenne
2 tablespoons creamy peanut
  butter
3 pounds white-fleshed fish, cut in
  2-inch squares

Again reach for the Dutch oven, add the oil and sauté the onions over medium heat. When they are limp, add the stock, tomato paste, ginger, curry, cayenne and peanut butter. Cook 5 minutes to blend flavors.

At this point you could cool the sauce and wait for the fish to be caught, or take it out on the boat with you. When you have the fish, add it to the pot and simmer it, covered, for 15 to 20 minutes. Turn the fish several times during this period and stop cooking as soon as the fish flakes easily. Serves 4 to 6.

WIGGLING FISH TO DUCK SOUP

CHAPTER
11

Take one teaspoon beef bouillon, one teaspoon gelatin and a cup of hot water. Mix. You have just created a passable consommé. So what's difficult about soup? Nothing!

Though soup can be as simple or as complicated as you wish to make it, I'm not one to recommend the thin watery stuff that is sometimes served before dinner. I like a soup that has body. The heavenly bean soup Mother used to make still dominates my soup memory. A good soup can make a meal in itself.

Time out while I get a pot of soup started! Writing about it always stimulates that, and there is a jar of chicken stock in the refrigerator just waiting for action. It'll be a throw-together soup, a handful of lentils, a few beans, carrots, onions and a clove of garlic. I may add a handful of elbow macaroni and a few sunflower seeds later.

Just such a soup started the career of Ed Random (an alias). Ed was an avid outdoorsman. He'd rather hunt than work. In fact, he managed to quit most jobs or get fired from them at the beginning of hunting season each year.

Since he was a good worker, he always found another job, or was rehired, after the hunting season. In other words, Ed was neither a bum nor a rider on welfare. He simply loved hunting.

When he was thirty-five, he finally found the ideal job, working as a guide for an Alaskan outfitter. On the second day of the season at the hunting camp, he fell over a low cliff and injured his knee and ankle so badly he was unable to guide his assigned hunter. Told to go home, he was stubborn enough to stay in camp working as bull cook. At first he could handle only sitting-down jobs, but as his leg improved, he began to assist in the cooking. Within a week, the cook came down with a bad case of drunk. Then the cook was gone, and Ed finished the season cooking for the camp.

Ed started a new tradition in camp cooking. He always had a pot of good soup on the stove which anyone could dish up for himself at any time. Soon, Ed's throw-together, handful-of-this-and-that soup became very popular. In fact, a client, a businessman from Seattle, tried to hire Ed to cook for his family, but Ed's own family wouldn't think of moving and he had to refuse the job.

By the end of the hunting season, Ed knew that his injury had ended his days of climbing mountainous terrain to hunt sheep. He began to think of a change of careers and that winter took a food service course being offered by the community college in Anchorage.

His instructor didn't favor the handful-of-this-and-that method of cooking and set Ed on the path to real success as a chef. After Ed cooked one more year in the hunting camp, he was ready for other things. The beginning of the Alaska pipeline construction gave him the opportunity he wanted. He spent five years keeping hard-working bodies fed.

And today? Well, if you should be in Anchorage for a restaurant meal so good you wish to send your compliments to the chef, Ed may well have fixed your meal. If you like the soup, chances are even better that Ed is your chef. He still has fond memories of the soup that changed his life.

I **must also tell you** how a simple bowl of soup was the catalyst in the

KODIAK BORSCHT
#I and #II

A year of my youth was spent in the city of Kodiak on the island of the same name. Since then I've made many visits back to the area. The old Russian dish, borscht, was not unknown there. I had always assumed the word *borscht* meant *beet soup*. Recently, however, I was told *borscht* means only *soup*. So here's a couple of soup recipes.

Borscht #I
1 No. 303 can (16 to 17 oz.) beets,
    sliced or diced, with liquid
1 cup water
1/4 cup sugar
1 teaspoon lemon juice
1/2 cup sour cream

Pour beets and liquid in a blender. Add the water, sugar and lemon juice. Blend until smooth and pour into serving bowls. Chill in the refrigerator for 2 hours. At serving time add a heaping spoonful of sour cream to each serving of the cold soup. Do not mix in the cream. Serves 4 and is especially nice on a hot summer day.

Borscht #II
2 cups beets, peeled and shredded
    (or canned)
4 cups beef stock
1 cup shredded carrots
1 cup finely chopped onion
Salt and pepper
1 tablespoon butter
1 cup shredded cabbage
1 tablespoon lemon juice
1 cup sour cream

In your largest soup pot combine the beets, beef stock, carrots and onions. Salt and pepper to taste and cook for 20 minutes over medium heat. (Note: If you use canned beets, do not add until the last 5 minutes of the cooking time.)

Add butter and cabbage and cook another 20 minutes. Add lemon juice and stir.

Spoon into serving bowls and place a large gob of sour cream in the center of each bowl. Serves 4 to 6.

UNSUCCESSFUL FISHERMAN'S CHOWDER

One spring I was talked into going fishing too early in the season. Boating, I called it. I didn't expect to catch any fish, so I took with me the makings of a chowder.

1 9-ounce can tuna, packed in oil
1 onion, chopped
1/4 teaspoon oregano
3 cups water
2 potatoes, peeled and sliced thin
1 can tomato soup
1 teaspoon salt
Pepper
Dried parsley flakes

I fired up the Shipmate stove and slid a medium-sized pot onto it. I opened the can of tuna, drained the oil into the pan and sautéed the chopped onion till it was soft, crumbling the oregano over the top. I added 3 cups water, the salt and potatoes and cooked them 15 minutes. Then I added the tomato soup, flaked the tuna into the pan and cooked the mixture 5 minutes or more to blend the flavors.

We served the soup in large mugs with pepper and parsley sprinkled on top. It served 4 nicely. We thought fresh fish while we ate it but didn't catch a thing. I enjoyed the boating, though.

romance of Red Eye Dinnerham and Sheila Whitney.

Sheila worked in a cafe in Glennallen, on the Glenn Highway. You probably know the one. All the truckers stop there. One evening Sheila was dead tired. Not only did her feet hurt, but she'd also had truckers "up to here." Into this happy situation blew a rather loud truck driver known as Red Eye.

Red Eye sat on the stool closest to the kitchen to better look over the new stuff. Not the menu . . . Sheila! He loudly ordered a bowl of soup.

Sheila ladled a full bowl. As she turned to place it on the counter, she tripped, lost her balance and fell forward. Still she managed to hold the soup bowl level and spilled not a drop, though her thumb slipped down into the soup.

She pulled her thumb out of the soup and had it halfway to her mouth when Red

Eye's hand shot out like a striking snake and caught her hand in midair. Pulling her hand across the counter he said, "I'll be paying for a full bowl of soup and I want it all!" With that, he thrust the soup-covered thumb into his mouth.

The hand he'd captured was Sheila's left. With her right, her fist doubling en route, she swung at Red Eye's chin. The blow delivered a full 130 pounds of angry woman to the point just in front of his jaw hinge.

Red Eye's head snapped back and his body followed suit. When it reached the point of no return, he crashed backwards to the floor, landing on his head with a strange hollow sound.

The other drivers turned to see Sheila looking at her fist in wonder. They noticed Red Eye on the floor and went back to eating.

Red Eye might have lain there for hours but for the bull cook who ran out with a bucket of cold water and splashed him down.

When Red Eye was conscious again, Sheila leaned over the counter and said, "Your soup's getting cold, mister!"

A much-subdued Red Eye climbed back on his stool and finished his soup. Then Sheila, feeling slightly guilty, offered him the use of her nearby trailer to change his clothes. He accepted.

One week later Red Eye arrived at the cafe bearing a dozen roses and a changed attitude. Sheila served him soup without thumb.

Six trips later he proposed, right between the soup course and the special of the day. She thought it over while he finished dinner and then delivered her answer with a large slice of apple pie. . . . My kind of woman! Isn't food romantic?

I can't promise you a new career or a new romance if you follow these soup recipes, but I can promise good eating!

BODENBURG CREAM OF POTATO SOUP

I was really into making soup back in the days when our family was living near Bodenburg Butte in the Matanuska Valley. My favorite was clam chowder, but with eight of us in the family, the proportion of potatoes to clams became larger and larger. One son suggested that I rename the soup "potato chowder," so I tried leaving the clams out.

2 tablespoons butter or margarine
1 cup chopped onion
3 cups water
4 cups potatoes, peeled, diced to
        1/4-inch cubes
2 cups carrots, peeled, diced to
        1/4-inch cubes
1 teaspoon salt
1/8 teaspoon pepper
1 13-ounce can evaporated milk
1/2 teaspoon parsley

In a Dutch oven, over medium heat, melt the butter and sauté the onions until tender. Add water, potatoes, carrots, salt and pepper.

Bring to a boil and simmer for 20 minutes so that the vegetables are just done, not mushy. Stir in the can of milk and add the parsley. Heat the soup to just under a boil and serve. It will serve 4 to 6.

If you absolutely must, add a couple of cans of clams.

CONCORD BUTTERBALL SOUP

I'm one of those people who can never throw away a quantity of good stock, beef, chicken or fish. I put jars of the stuff in the refrigerator and am always looking for things to make with this liquid gold.

This simple and good recipe from a friend is very old. She claims it's been in her family for 200 years.

1-1/2 quarts chicken stock
8 slices white bread
1 egg
1/4 cup butter
1/2 teaspoon dried parsley
1/4 teaspoon salt

Pour the chicken stock into a large saucepan over medium heat and start it toward a boil.

Trim the crusts from the bread, break the bread into chunks and turn them into crumbs using a blender.

In a bowl combine the egg, butter, parsley, crumbs, and salt and mix until the contents can be formed into 3/4-inch balls. Make as many as the material allows.

Drop the balls into the boiling chicken stock and simmer for 10 minutes. They will rise to the top when done. Ladle into soup bowls. Serves 4 to 6.

KITCHEN SINK SOUP

I have been accused of throwing everything but the kitchen sink into my soups. In fact, one child insinuated that a harmless piece of eggshell he found in his soup was a chip of enamel off the sink.

The following soup contains no egg, eggshells or sink. But it's good anyway.

3 tablespoons vegetable oil
1 cup chopped onion
1/2 cup chopped celery
1 clove garlic, minced
1-1/2 teaspoons salt
1/2 teaspoon rosemary
4 cups assorted chopped
    vegetables, such as carrots,
    cauliflower, peas, turnips,
    green beans, cabbage,
    zucchini
1-1/2 cups sliced tomatoes, fresh or
    canned
3-1/2 cups beef stock
1/2 cup pasta—macaroni,
    spaghetti, or noodles
2 cups toasted bread cubes
1 teaspoon dried parsley
1/2 cup Parmesan cheese
Pepper

Put the oil in a Dutch oven and place it over medium heat. Add the onions, celery and garlic and sauté. When they are tender, stir in the salt and rosemary.

Add the vegetables and stir for 5 minutes over the heat to blend flavors. Add the beef stock, bring the liquid to a boil, lower heat, and simmer for 10 minutes.

Add the pasta and cook another 10 to 15 minutes until it's tender.

During this last cooking period, toss the bread cubes, parsley and cheese together and set aside.

Serve in deep bowls and garnish with seasoned bread cubes. Yield: 4 to 6 servings.

POTATO AND CHEESE SOUP

This recipe from my file is in my mother's handwriting and bears marginal notes that lead me to believe it came from my French great-grandmother. No doubt it was brought here when the family moved from France to Canada well over 100 years ago.

3 cups beef stock (or 4 bouillon
cubes and 3 cups water)
1 cup chopped onion
2 cups cooked, mashed potatoes
(leftovers?)
1/2 cup milk
4 ounces Cheddar cheese, shredded
Salt and pepper

In your Dutch oven, over medium heat, combine the stock and onions and simmer for 10 minutes. Add the potatoes, stir well and simmer another 15 minutes. Season to taste. Add the milk and cheese and simmer, without bringing to a boil, for another 15 minutes.

Ladle into 4 soup bowls. Serve with croutons. *Bon appetit!*

COQUENHENA DUCK SOUP

In my youth — before aircraft were used to fly hunters to remote areas — a duck hunt was a many-day event. We traveled by slow boat to the Copper River Flats. The early birds of the hunt were usually consumed there. This soup was my first meal at Coquenhena Slough.

4 fresh ducks, plucked and cut into
pieces
12 carrots, cut in chunks
4 cups chopped onion
2 cups chopped celery
1 tablespoon salt
1/4 teaspoon pepper
6 bay leaves
1 cup pitted dried prunes
1/4 cup raisins
1-1/2 cups vinegar
1/2 cup sugar

Place duck in a large pot with enough water to cover. Bring to a boil and skim the surface. Add celery, carrots, onions, salt, pepper and bay leaves and simmer until duck is almost done, about 40 minutes — less for a young duck; more if the duck is old. Add prunes and raisins and cook 5 minutes more.

Combine the vinegar and sugar and add to the pot. Continue cooking until duck is tender. Serve directly from pot to deep plates or bowls. The soup will serve 4 to 6, depending on the size of the ducks.

CREAM OF MOOSEBURGER SOUP

Back in the good old days, there were times when our Deepfreeze became awfully empty looking. The moose that looked big enough to last forever had been scarfed up by two adults and six youngsters. At these periods my mind usually turned to soup, which can stretch a little meat to feed a lot of people well.

3 slices bacon
2 cups sliced onion
1 pound ground moose, beef,
*   caribou or available meat*
4 cups water
2 teaspoons salt
1/4 teaspoon pepper
1 tablespoon parsley
1 cup shredded carrot
1/2 cup uncooked elbow macaroni
1/2 cup tomato juice
2 tablespoons margarine or butter
2 tablespoons flour
1 cup milk

Fry the bacon until crisp in a Dutch oven over medium heat. Remove it from the pan and sauté the onions in the grease for 5 minutes. Add the ground beef, stirring while it browns to break it into small pieces. Add the water, salt, pepper, parsley and carrots. Simmer for 10 minutes. Add the macaroni and tomato juice and simmer for another 15 minutes.

In another pan, melt the butter and add flour to make into a roux; then carefully add the milk. Stir and cook until the liquid thickens. Pour this liquid into the soup and stir for another 5 minutes. Crumble bacon and sprinkle some over each serving. Yield: 4 servings.

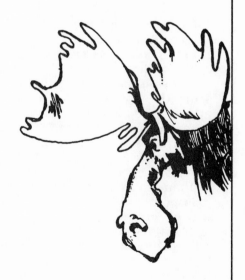

BLODGETT BARBECUE SAUCE

In another chapter (Spareribs to Travel), I described how to prepare spareribs for picnics. This is the way my father-in-law prepared them in advance for occasions when the whole family went to Blodgett Lake for a picnic. He introduced me to this flavorful barbecue sauce, good for basting during cooking and for serving in a sauceboat with finished ribs.

1 cup finely chopped onion
2 tablespoons vegetable oil
1 cup tomato ketchup
1/4 cup lemon juice
1 tablespoon brown sugar
1 tablespoon Worcestershire
1/4 teaspoon dry mustard
1 cup beef or pork stock
1-1/4 teaspoons salt
1/4 teaspoon cayenne
1/4 teaspoon pepper
1/4 teaspoon celery seed

In a saucepan over medium heat, sauté the onions in oil for a few minutes. Add ketchup, lemon juice, sugar, Worcestershire sauce and dry mustard. Mix well and add stock. Simmer for 20 minutes. Add salt, cayenne, pepper and celery seed and continue to simmer for 10 minutes. It is permissible to thin the sauce with water if needed.

The finished sauce can be used immediately, or kept refrigerated or frozen until needed. Try it on beef, too.

GAKONA DRY MOOSE SAUCE

The moose that is taken late in the season and destined to feed many Alaskan families is often a dry and lean animal. To the lovers of fat beef, the late-season moose isn't much of a treat.

While living in Glennallen one winter, we learned from a family in Gakona how to make a sauce to eliminate some of the problem. It's good on *fat* moose or beef, too.

1/2 cup rendered beef fat
1 cup fresh chopped tomatoes or
*   stewed tomatoes*
1 cup minced onion
1/2 cup dried green onion, plumped
*   in a small amount of water*
Salt and pepper
1-1/2 cups water
1 4-ounce can mushroom stems
*   and pieces*

In a frying pan over medium heat bring the fat to hot. Combine all the vegetables except mushrooms in a bowl and salt and pepper to taste. Pour them into the hot grease and sauté for 3 minutes. Add water and bring to a boil. Cook for 10 minutes, stirring occasionally. Drain the mushrooms, add them to the sauce and heat for another 2 minutes. Add extra liquid if the mixture appears too dry.

Serve either on or beside the meat.

ALASKAN SAUCES MAGNIFICO

CHAPTER
12

I'm a collector of sauces, not the kind that are hoked up to cover badly prepared food, but sauces that contribute something more to the already delectable taste of good food.

During my fifty years of travel in Alaska, all too often I've been served a sauce designed to hide something. Such sauces are usually called "gravy" and vary more in color than in taste. A piece of beef needing help for many reasons will be hidden under a heavy brown stain; pork, under red; chicken is given the honor of a sickly yellow. Once I was served scrambled boat eggs under the same yellow gravy, and a hunk of freezer-burned halibut . . . well, let us not discuss that. The memory is enough to send me searching in the kitchen for something to remove the after-taste. Instead, let me tell you a love story.

I never knew Mike Redoubt, but I knew his story. He fell in love with Mildred Faith Hansen on the day he first tasted her famous fish sauce served on a fresh king salmon steak.

Mildred Hansen knew full well what she was doing when she slipped that plate of salmon steak to Mike. At the tender age of twenty-six, she was already twice widowed. Her first husband she had attracted with the full use of her considerable wiles. To list them all might be considered chauvinistic. How well Mildred filled a bikini is still talked about. Her smile, revealing rows of perfect, white teeth, melted all male resistance. And, too-good-to-be-true as it may seem (like adding whipped cream to pumpkin pie), she was a fine cook.

Her first husband, Ed Timberman, was

a fisherman. He went to the Aleutian Islands aboard a crabber to get rich. Instead, the crabber and all its crew disappeared from the face of the earth in a violent storm. Ed's insurance made Mildred a wealthy widow. But she wanted a husband.

We should not be too hard on her because the husband she found, Ralph Hansen, belonged to another woman. That deterrent aside, Mildred and Ralph were married one summer day. Only a month later, Ralph, too, died when his fishing boat was lost at sea.

Now Mike Redoubt, Ralph's best friend, stepped into the picture to comfort the widow, by now doubly wealthy with another large insurance payoff. Soon she had picked Mike for Husband Number Three.

But Mike, still thinking of Mildred as his friend's wife, didn't respond to her first overtures as she expected. Fat chance he had to keep up the resistance.

Just three weeks to the day after he held her hand at the funeral, he was invited to her home for dinner. Mourning was over.

Mike arrived dressed in his only suit, flowers in hand — to honor his old friend, of course.

There is no use imagining the before-dinner conversation because the real action began with the king salmon steak and Mildred's special sauce.

Mike took one look at the sauce-covered salmon and nearly gagged. But Mildred flashed her lovely smile at him in encouragement, and he tried the first bite. It proved to be fantastic.

"Magnificent!" he said, smiling across the table at his new love.

The remainder of the story is simple. They married, she tied well the silken cord and would not allow Mike to go fishing any more. Instead, they created the M&M Fish Sauce Company.

MEIERS STEAK SAUCE

One of the old roadhouses, Meiers, was still in operation when I was first assigned to the Glennallen Station by the Alaska Highway Patrol. It was located about halfway between Sourdough and Paxton roadhouses. I stopped there often on my northern patrol. Meiers served a good meat sauce which I have tried to duplicate in this recipe.

1/4 pound butter
1/4 teaspoon garlic powder
1 teaspoon finely chopped onion
1 teaspoon dried dill leaves,
    crumbled
1 teaspoon lemon juice
1/4 teaspoon coarsely ground
    pepper
1 teaspoon paprika

In a small saucepan over medium heat, melt the butter. Stir in remaining ingredients and simmer lightly for 10 minutes.

Spread the thick sauce over any red meat — hamburger, roast beef or moose.

ANNDELTNA SAUCE

As much as I enjoy turning out a delectable sauce, I'm sometimes rushed. Such as when I have a hot sequence in the typewriter and forget it's close to dinner time. So I need a hurry-up sauce to dress up the evening's vegetables. Here's a quicky.

1/4 cup butter
1 cup finely chopped onion
1/4 cup milk
1 10- to 12-ounce can Cheddar
    cheese soup

The butter goes into a saucepan over medium heat. The onions are sautéed until they are tender. The soup and milk are added and stirred continuously until the sauce is heated through. Do not boil.

Serve hot over green vegetables such as asparagus, broccoli or zucchini. Or try it on scrambled eggs some morning. But whenever you serve it, hide the soup can. Never admit you used that. Heavens!

And I will never admit Anndeltna is a placename with a name but no place. But you can stop searching your map now.

Can I provide you the recipe? Unfortunately not. Even their son, Ralph, who was in the army with me, did not know the secret of the sauce. Besides, you can see how dangerous it would be to share it.

Not all the sauces in this chapter are my own creations. The file comes from many sources. A couple of sauces came from an Englishman I'll call only "Magnifico." Actually, the title is his own, and he has an ambition to match it. He wishes someday to create the perfect sauce. He searches for it, even today, but I am convinced that he will not recognize the perfect sauce when and if he finds it. Perhaps the search and experiment are more important to him than perfection.

He has found several recipes valuable enough to keep under lock and key. One must be able to trade something of equal value to gain one of these recipes. I have tasted sixteen of his recipes and now I, too, have one ambition — to obtain one of his recipes by fair trade. Talk about shooting for the moon! (But they made it, didn't they?)

A few years ago I conned Magnifico into going with me on a ptarmigan hunt up in the Talkeetna Mountains. The shotgun he took must have cost a thousand pounds sterling. I'm sure my old Winchester pump gun was embarrassed to be in the same gun rack with his double. In fact, to get even with me, it missed the first three shots I fired from it.

Magnifico had a wonderful time hunting what he kept calling "upland bird." I had always thought of ptarmigan as a hillside bird. He corrected me and soon had his limit, whereupon he became mellow enough to invite Connie and me to his house for dinner . . . as soon as he had "properly aged the birds."

With hopes of a new recipe, Connie and I arrived at his house on the specified day. There was a reasonable delay in the living room while we sipped wine, and then dinner was announced. The soup was mainly bean sprouts and bouillon, delicate and delicious. The salad was, again, mainly sprouts and a delicate dressing I couldn't identify (nor was I given the recipe).

The main course was ptarmigan breasts. They had been boned, pounded with much skill and cooked with a tender touch. They were arranged on the serving platter and covered with a pale yellow sauce. There was more of the sauce in a sauceboat beside the meat. I helped myself with skill and daring equal to the meal.

Ptarmigan is usually tough and wild tasting. This meat was as tender as anything I have ever eaten. The first bite was heavenly. The sauce *had* to be the one he'd searched for all these years. It was by far the best bird I had ever tasted.

At the end of the meal he delivered to me the recipe. It was neatly typed on monogrammed stationery. Impressive.

I've since tried the sauce on other fowl and on fish and have always found it excellent, though never quite like it was that night. (But, then, he cooked the bird by a recipe that remains secret.)

KODIAK BEEF SAUCE

The excellent beef produced on Kodiak Island certainly deserves a sauce named after it. I have here a recipe adapted from another island's cooking that will do nicely: English Yorkshire pudding. Take the time to try this with your next beef or moose roast.

1/8 teaspoon salt
1/4 cup flour
1/2 teaspoon baking powder
1 cup milk
1 egg, beaten
1/2 cup drippings from the roast

Sift the salt, flour and baking powder into a medium-sized bowl. In another bowl combine the milk and egg. Add a third of the milk mixture to the flour bowl. Beat until the batter is smooth and then blend in the remainder to make a soft dough.

Pour the roast drippings into an 8 x 8-inch square baking pan and add the dough to the pan. Bake in a 375° oven for 25 minutes. Remove and cut into squares. Serve with the roast beef. Yes, it's a bit more solid than the sauces you may be used to, but the taste is grand. This recipe usually serves 4.

MAGIE'S GINGER LEMON SAUCE

I've told you Magnifico's story already. "Magie" was a nickname that grew during a number of hunting camps we shared in later years.

1/2 cup sugar
3/4 cup spring water, or at least water without chlorine
2 teaspoons cornstarch
2 tablespoons lemon juice*
3/4 cup dry sherry
1/2 teaspoon ground ginger
2 tablespoons soy sauce
2 teaspoons chicken bouillon granules

In a medium-sized bowl combine the sugar, water and cornstarch. Mix well and add the lemon juice, sherry, ginger, soy sauce and chicken bouillon granules. Mix again.

Pour the liquid into a saucepan. Cook over medium heat, stirring constantly while the sauce comes to a boil and thickens. Serve as soon as possible.

This sauce is excellent ladled over poached, baked or pan-broiled chicken or fish. My favorite way of using it is the recipe on page 94, Chicken Chicken Ginger Lemon.

*Using lime juice, for Magie's Ginger Lime Sauce, makes a pleasant taste variation.

UN-I-MAK SAUCE

This sauce has nothing whatever to do with Unimak Island. *I* named it Un-Mac Sauce, as in Un-Cola, but Connie argued the title wasn't Alaskan enough.

The idea for the sauce originated when I ate at a certain fast food place that brags about its hamburgers on a sesame seed bun with a special sauce. . . . I felt challenged. I knew I could invent a sauce as good, maybe better. Try this one and make up your own mind. But, caution; use of the sauce may make you subject to un-i-mak attacks.

1 cup sour cream
1/2 cup sweet pickle relish
1/4 teaspoon celery salt
1/8 teaspoon black pepper

Combine the ingredients in a small bowl and chill. Spread over your next hamburger and make the test yourself.

HONEY SOY SAUCE

This interesting sauce was first served to me hot, over a bowl of freshly cooked and shelled shrimp. I've tried it over fish, cooked crab and even over boned chicken.

1/2 cup soy sauce
3 tablespoons honey
1/2 teaspoon salt
1/8 teaspoon pepper
1 clove garlic, finely minced

Combine all the ingredients in a small saucepan and heat while stirring. Serve hot.

POOR MAN'S CRAB SAUCE

The Matanuska Valley is too far from the sea and my old crab traps. The market price of the crawly creatures has almost eliminated them from my diet, and I miss having crab on my dinner plate. Since I can't kick the crab habit entirely, when I run onto a sauce like this one, I *must* have the recipe.

1 6-ounce can crab meat
1 10- to 12-ounce can mushroom
    soup
1/4 cup light cream
1 teaspoon lemon juice
2 tablespoons sherry

Pick through the crab for shell or membrane. In a saucepan, over medium heat, combine the soup and cream and heat to just under a boil. Add lemon juice, sherry and crab meat. Return the sauce to just under a boil, stirring gently.

Serve the sauce over rice, noodles, scrambled eggs or anything else your imagination can contrive.

INTERNATIONAL ORANGE SAUCE

The Alaska Road Commission, which cared for Alaska's roads before Statehood, painted everything a color known as "international orange." Everything that moved, that is, including some personnel (at least the painters), I suspect.

The first time I saw this sauce I recognized the familiar color. It was proudly displayed on a rainbow trout. The sauce, I mean.

6 egg yolks
1/4 cup sugar
1/2 cup vinegar
Juice of 3 oranges
1 tablespoon grated orange peel
Juice of 1 lemon
1 tablespoon grated lemon peel
1-1/4 cups white wine
Salt

Assemble your double boiler, combine the ingredients in the top pan and mix well. Cook over hot water, stirring, until the sauce thickens. Salt to taste.

Serve sauce hot over freshwater fish or seafood.

CHUNG'S IMPROVED SOY SAUCE

On a visit to Ketchikan I discovered a Chinese restaurant whose chef really knew how to steam rice. A large bowl of it was served with every order and, accompanying it for seasoning, was a small pitcher of excellent soy sauce, the best I ever tasted. I have finally found a recipe that comes close to matching that soy sauce.

1 cup beef stock, strained clear
1/2 cup soy sauce (your brand)
1 tablespoon cornstarch

Heat the beef stock in a saucepan over medium heat. Combine soy sauce and cornstarch in a small bowl. When it is well mixed, pour slowly into the hot beef stock. Keep stirring to prevent lumps from forming and cook for 5 minutes.

Serve the sauce as hot as possible to go with steamed rice, or try it over egg foo yong.

MAGNIFICO'S ENGLISH BAY SAUCE

I mentioned the sauces of my friend Magnifico earlier. This one was named in honor of a memorable trip he made to English Bay, down near Homer, on the Kenai Peninsula. He never told me her name. But he gave me her recipe.

1/4 cup minced onion
1 tablespoon butter
1 cup chicken stock
1/4 cup orange juice
1/4 cup lime juice
2 tablespoons Worcestershire
2 tablespoons cornstarch
1 tablespoon water
1 tablespoon currant jelly

In a saucepan sauté the onions in butter over medium heat. Add stock, juices, and Worcestershire and cook, stirring, until smooth, about 5 minutes. Combine the cornstarch and water and slowly add to the hot sauce. Continue stirring until the sauce thickens. Add the currant jelly after you have turned off the heat, stirring it into the finished sauce.

Serve over chicken, ham or even pork chops. It can make excellent meats even better. *Magnifico!*

CURRY CASSEROLE SAUCE

I first tasted this sauce in a casserole of mountain sheep, rice and a few vegetables. It was so delicious, I flattered the recipe right out of the hostess. It's useful with any meat casserole.

3 tablespoons butter
2 tablespoons all-purpose flour
1-1/2 cups milk
1 tablespoon curry powder
1 teaspoon salt
1/4 teaspoon pepper

Melt the butter in a saucepan over medium heat. Stir in the flour to make a roux. Remove from the heat and carefully stir in the milk. Add curry, salt and pepper, return to heat, and cook slowly, without boiling, until the sauce thickens.

Add the sauce to a casserole before cooking or ladle it over cooked meats at serving time.

MERINGUED EGGS

Hidden in my mother's notes I found a recipe that clearly demonstrates there is nothing like an egg. You think you know all about it and then discover a *new* way of cooking it that was thought up 100 years ago. You will want to try this one for sure.

4 slices bread, whole-wheat
    preferred
Butter
4 eggs
4 very thin slices of ham or cheese

Start by buttering 1 side of each slice of bread and slipping the bread under a broiler. Toast 1 side only.

While the bread is toasting, separate the eggs. Keep the yolks separated from each other in half shells. Combine the whites in a bowl and whip them until they cling to the sides of the bowl.

Save the toast from the oven and turn the heat down to 375°. Then butter the untoasted side of the bread. Place it toasted side down on a cookie sheet. Lay a slice of ham on each piece. Divide the egg whites and spread on the ham. Form a hollow in the egg whites on each piece and slip a yolk into the hollow.

Bake in a 375° oven for 15 minutes, or until the meringue is a delicate brown. Serve at once. Yield: 4 servings.

ALAGANIK SALMON OMELET

In the days I wandered the Copper River Flats with my brother and dad, I heard the name Alaganik mentioned often. When I asked about the place, a family joke developed. No matter what I asked or did, one of them would say, "Hey! What can you expect from a kid who's never been to Alaganik?" I've still never been there, but we caught lots of salmon not too far away. (I guess!)

1 cup cooked salmon or a
    7-1/2-ounce can of salmon,
    well drained
1/3 cup fish stock (or liquid from the
    can plus water needed)
1 teaspoon parsley
1/2 teaspoon salt
1 tablespoon finely minced onion
Pepper
Oregano, ground or crumbled
6 eggs, beaten
2 tablespoons butter

Combine fish stock, parsley, salt, onion and a dash, each, of pepper and oregano. Add eggs and mix well.

Melt butter in a 10-inch frying pan, pour in the egg mixture and cook over low heat for 3 or 4 minutes. Flake the fish over half the cooking egg. When a knife can be inserted and comes out clean, score the halfway mark and fold omelet in half. Cook 2 or 3 more minutes and slide out onto a warm plate. Yield: 4 servings.

TRUCK EGGS

CHAPTER
13

If you have the image of an egg cracking and a tiny eighteen-wheeler rolling out, you've missed the point of this chapter title. (But it's a cute little truck, isn't it?)

The eggs that arrived in the Alaska of my youth came to us, like all produce, by steamship, and were known in my family as "boat eggs." As they were sometimes long in storage, they aged into flavorsome things — even into eggs with body (a chick's) and fragrance (better known as *stink*). These were the eggs I grew up with.

Today, most eggs used in Alaska arrive in highway vans which either roll up the Alaska Highway or off a ship in the port of Anchorage. And, hey! These truck eggs are fresh, only ten refrigerated days out of the chicken.

Nowadays, if you want to find a dozen rotten eggs to throw at an actor or politician, you have to plan ahead to condition a few yourself. I have a dozen set aside and might spare you a few if your political opinions are similar to mine. For egging on actors, you are on your own.

Luckily, I live in the Matanuska Valley where fresh farm eggs are available. Direct from the chicken to me with a minimum of delay, they arrive in my home with that delicate, fresh taste still evident. I love these eggs!

In fact, the pursuit of greater freshness has several times brought me to the edge of folly: I have considered getting a flock of chickens. To keep myself from doing such a foolish thing, twice a year I visit Adam Grath's chicken ranch.

Adam started small with a tiny building and a dozen laying chickens. Oh yes, and a rooster. Adam, too, was a fresh-egg lover. I know, because once he gave me a dozen eggs right out from under the chickens. Never again, however. The freshness of those eggs was almost more than my sanity could bear, and I refuse to allow myself any further temptation to keep chickens.

MARNIE SCOTCH EGGS

I first tasted Scotch eggs aboard the cannery tender *Marnie*. The skipper, my brother, had been kidding the cook about the way he fixed eggs. The next Sunday, while we were at anchor and the cook could work with some degree of safety, he prepared this recipe.

6 hard-cooked eggs
2 tablespoons milk
1 raw egg, beaten
1/2 cup bread crumbs
1 pound ground pork sausage

In a medium-sized bowl combine the milk and the raw egg. Put the bread crumbs in another bowl. Start your deep-fat fryer heating toward 450°.

Divide the sausage into sixths. Wrap each hard-cooked egg in sausage meat, being sure that all the egg is covered. Dip the sausaged egg into the raw-egg batter and roll it in the bread crumbs until covered.

Ease the sausaged eggs into the hot fryer and cook until golden brown, about 5 minutes.

Serve hot to 3 or more.

Adam enjoyed his small flock and the eggs. Then, alas, he started giving fresh eggs to his family, at first only to the single children; then to the married couples with children; and finally to some grown-up grandchildren. His small flock grew to two dozen chickens, then to four dozen, and he still wasn't getting enough to keep any eggs for himself.

The chicken coops grew with the number of hens (still with their one happy rooster). Today Adam no longer hunts or fishes. He is a slave to his chickens, not to mention the grandchildren's children.

I'll *buy* my eggs, thank you. Do you have any idea how many children and grandchildren I have? I'm a typewriter slave and happy with the condition.

My friend, Mel, has the nerve to rate beer above the egg, but I get even. I always break the yolk of "his egg" when I fry eggs. He doesn't deserve a nicely fried-in-butter egg. Maybe he doesn't deserve eggs at all. He *boils* his eggs for fifteen minutes . . . ugh!

Quite definitely I appreciate eggs more than that and treat them to the dignity they deserve. A 3-minute egg is carefully timed. Never is it left in the water for 200 seconds. Before I make a soufflé, I yell, "Scat!" and I can feel the temperature drop ten degrees as my family all scamper out the doors too hastily to close them again.

Where did I learn to break Mel's egg for spite? I'll tell you.

I first met Edward R. Murdock, also known as Egg Island Ed, in my folks' living room. Later I found out what earned him his nickname, how he'd stuck the cannery tender *Moose* high and dry on Egg Island for more than three tides.

My father had sailed his own tender past Ed's embarrassment and later brought the man home for a mug-up that stretched into dinner time. After dinner the elders got to telling stories in the living room, and I stayed to listen.

Both my dad and older brother, Ken, had told true stories slightly creatively to make them better listening. Now it was Ed's turn.

"Did you know I hold the record for the greatest number of eggs ever fried at one time?" he began.

Dad assured him we hadn't known and asked to be enlightened. Mother went right to the point and asked, "How many?" Then we relaxed and listened to his story.

"I was the cook in the Kenai camp during the construction of the Alaska Northern Railroad from Seward to Kern. That's the railroad the federal government took over and continued as The Alaska Railroad. Originally it just headed for the mines in the Girdwood area.

(See? It is a cute little truck.)

"Al Peters started the whole egg-frying thing by claiming the egg-frying championship for his Sunshine camp. He had whipped out twenty eggs in his biggest frying pan.

"Mike Swift at the Seward camp got in the act by using the largest prospector's gold pan he could find. He was able to fry up fifty eggs at one time. But he was too damned smug about his victory to suit me. He knew the gold pan was the biggest pan in Alaska. He was sure that his record would stand," Ed explained.

We all waited for Ed to finish the second cup of coffee Mother had poured. After the last swallow, he took a big breath and began again.

"My first problem was finding a pan bigger than Mike's. It had to be small enough to fit on my camp range and still huge enough to grasp forever the record. I talked over my problem with Greg Ironsmith, the blacksmith down in Seward. He was sure he could solve the problem.

"He cut the end out of a fifty-five-gallon oil drum, leaving a lip of some three inches. To the bottom of the new pan he welded a circular piece of boiler plate. This was to draw and spread the heat evenly enough to fry the eggs. The finished pan was too heavy for one man to lift, so he welded a handle on either side. At last we were ready.

"I invited both Al Peters and Mike Swift to breakfast on the morning of the great test. Another twenty-five or so hungry witnesses showed up.

"For the half-hour before cooking I had been busy breaking eggs into a large bowl. The total now stood at 100. With the witnesses forming a half-circle around the stove, my bull cook and I lifted the great pan onto the stove. I poured in a pint of bacon grease and spread it with a four-inch paintbrush as the pan heated.

"Then we tipped the bowl of eggs

EGG ISLAND CASSEROLE

The only thing Egg Island and this casserole have in common is that they disappear at high tide. That is, on the days when dinner and high tide happen at the same time. What more do you want?

4 hard-cooked eggs, sliced
*   lengthwise*
1/4 cup butter
1/4 cup flour
2 cups milk
1 cup shredded Cheddar cheese
1 cup diced ham, dried beef, or
*   other cooked meat*
2 tablespoons Worcestershire

Melt the butter in a saucepan over medium heat and stir in the flour to make a roux. Remove from the heat and stir in the milk. Replace on the heat and stir until sauce thickens. Add the shredded cheese and stir until blended.

Remove from the heat and add the ham and Worcestershire. Mix well.

Place the eggs, cut side down, on the bottom of a buttered casserole dish and pour the ham mixture over them. Bake in a preheated 350° oven for 15 minutes.

Serve with buttered toast. Yield: 4 servings.

HOPE EGG-AND-SAUSAGE CASSEROLE

A few years ago I went to the community of Hope, which sits on the south shore of Turnagain Arm of Cook Inlet. I was looking for a witness and found both him and a mug-up.* In fact the mug-up lengthened into lunch. This is what was served:

4 eggs, beaten well
1 pound bulk sausage, browned
*   and crumbled*
1 9-ounce can cream-style corn
1 cup bread crumbs
1 teaspoon salt
1/4 teaspoon pepper
Ketchup

In a medium-sized bowl combine the eggs, browned sausage, corn and crumbs. Mix well, add salt and pepper and mix again. Put the mixture into a casserole dish evenly. Spread a light covering of ketchup over the top.

Set the casserole in a shallow pan of water in an oven preheated to 350°. Bake for 1 hour.

The casserole handles 4 nicely.

See page 146.

carefully into the pan. Now the special effort that I had put into leveling the stove paid off. The eggs spread out evenly in the pan. I added a bit more wood to the fire and glanced at Al and Mike. I enjoyed watching them count eggs.

"As the eggs cooked I organized my eaters into 'soft cooked' first in line and 'well done' later. I served directly from the pan to the line of witnesses with their plates. I eased the last two eggs to Mike's plate. One egg was broken! I told him, 'I'm sorry, Mike, I broke your egg.'

"Mike answered, 'You beat me fair and square, Ed, but how did you know that it was my yolk you had broken out of a hundred eggs?'

"And that is how I won the record for the most eggs fried in one pan," Ed said.

Into the silence that followed Ed's story, my voice was heard asking, "How did you know it was his yolk?"

My family never let me forget the blunder. Forever afterwards, if one yolk was broken in a frying pan full of eggs, that was "my egg." Now when *I'm* cooking, you can be sure that any egg yolk that is broken is "your egg" or Mel's if he's around.

I think you'll find some surprising egg recipes in this chapter. Try them all with the freshest eggs you can get. If you start an egg farm, let me know. I will visit twice a year, or maybe more often if you have many grandchildren to feed.

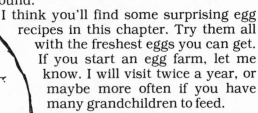

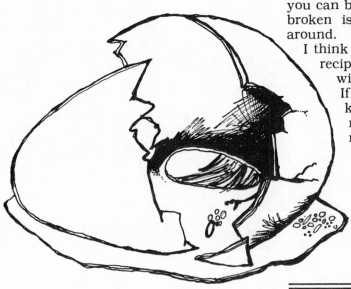

EGGS COLONIAL
(twice poached)

Until last fall I thought I knew every way to cook eggs. I was proven wrong when, for lunch, I was served Eggs Colonial.

My host took already-poached eggs from the refrigerator, heated and served them. I was fascinated by the method and I think you will be, too. It is an excellent way to prepare eggs for a crowd in advance and still manage to serve them delicately cooked, with little last-minute hassle.

Step 1: Pre-poaching eggs

Start with eggs at room temperature. Now bring a pan of water — enough to cover a single layer of eggs by 1 inch — to a rapid boil. Into it place the eggs, still in their shells, one at a time. Begin timing when the first egg goes into the water and allow each egg to be in the water 8 seconds. Then carefully and quickly remove the eggs in the same order you put them in. Or, simply pre-poach each egg, separately, for 8 seconds. Doing it that way will only cost you a few minutes, even if you're pre-poaching 2 dozen eggs.

Step 2: Poaching the eggs

Fill a nonstick frying pan with water to 1-1/2 inches deep. Heat. When the water comes just to the boil, reduce the heat so that bubbles rise to the surface of the water only once in a while. Break the pre-poached eggs into it *gently*, adding only as many at one time as can be kept apart. Already heat-set, each egg will keep its shape in the water. Cook from 3 to 5 minutes, to your preference.

Step 3: Stopping the cooking

With a slotted spoon, lift poached eggs from the water — again, in the order you put them in — and slide them immediately into ice-cold water.

Step 4: Storing poached eggs

Cover the eggs, still in the ice-water bath, and refrigerate until needed. Up to 24 hours is okay.

Step 5: Reheating to serve

To serve the eggs warm, slip them into a bowl well filled with hot water — *not* hot enough to cook them any further; even hot tap water will do the warming job — for 5 to 10 minutes. Drain and serve. Maybe on toast with Béarnaise sauce?

DILLINGHAM DILLED EGGS

Once I could brag that I had been in every bar in a state twice as big as Texas. But alas, when I retired the number of bars kept increasing. Now there are many I haven't visited. In a Dillingham bar, a while back, I saw pickled eggs. I asked for the recipe.

12 hard-cooked eggs, shelled
3/4 cup spring water or water
*   without chlorine*
1 clove garlic, minced
1/4 teaspoon mustard seed or
*   dry mustard*
1 teaspoon dill seed, bruised
2 teaspoons salt
1-1/4 cups white vinegar
1 onion, sliced

Bring the water, garlic, mustard, dill seed, salt and vinegar to a boil over medium heat. Reduce the heat and simmer for 10 minutes.

Meanwhile pack a wide-mouthed quart jar with alternate layers of eggs and onions. When the jar is full, pour the heated liquid slowly over all. It should cover the eggs. Add liquid if necessary (or eat an egg).

Cover the jar with aluminum foil and a rubber band. Chill at least 3 days before serving.

These eggs will keep 2 weeks hidden in the refrigerator or about 20 minutes sitting in plain view on the back bar.

RAMEKIN EGGS LORRAINE

A lady from Michigan sent me this recipe noting that it was "sorta' French!" Now I have only four ramekins so I reduced the recipe to fill that number. Feel free to expand as needed.

4 slices Canadian bacon or ham
4 thin slices Swiss cheese,
*   approximately 3 x 3-inch*
*   squares*
4 fresh eggs
Salt and pepper
1/4 cup sour cream

Place a slice of Canadian bacon in each buttered ramekin. Add a slice of cheese and break an egg over the cheese. Salt and pepper to taste, then cover with sour cream.

Bake in a 400° oven for 15 to 20 minutes, until the egg white is set.

Serve in the ramekins, with whole-wheat toast and lots of coffee. Serves 4.

NOVA SCOTIA EGGS

I'm assuming that this recipe came from Nova Scotia with my grandmother. The recipe is in my mother's hand but her notes indicate it came from her mother-in-law. I've never seen the recipe anywhere else. It's a way to serve six eggs to four people, with no one feeling slighted.

1 cup shredded Cheddar cheese
2 tablespoons butter
1/2 cup cream or undiluted
*   evaporated milk*
1 tablespoon prepared mustard
1/2 teaspoon salt
Pepper
6 eggs, slightly beaten

Begin with a 9 x 9-inch square, nonstick baking pan. Spread the shredded cheese over the bottom and dot with butter.

Combine the cream, mustard, salt and pepper to taste, and pour half of the mixture over the cheese.

Carefully pour the beaten eggs over the layer of cream in the pan. Then add the rest of the cream on top.

Bake in a preheated 325° oven for 25 minutes. Serve immediately. Yield: 4 servings.

SMITH POINT EGGS

Along the northern reaches of the Copper River Delta, there is a point with the common name, Smith. When we lived and worked there many long years ago, this was one of Mother's breakfast specialties.

1 15-ounce can corned beef hash
1/2 cup ketchup
1/2 cup minced onion
1/4 teaspoon salt
Pepper
1/4 cup water
4 eggs, fresh as possible

In a medium-sized, covered, frying pan, mix the hash, ketchup, onion, salt, water and pepper to taste. Smooth the surface, cover, and simmer over medium heat for 10 minutes. Uncover and make 4 egg-sized indentations in the hash. Break a raw egg into each hole. Return the cover and cook the eggs to the degree of doneness you like. This breakfast will serve from 2 to 4, depending on how hard the diners intend to work that morning.

BEAVER CREEK RHUBARB UPSIDE-DOWN CAKE

Only last year, on the banks of Beaver Creek, down on the Kenai Peninsula, I was seduced. By a cake, I quickly add. I'm not a great rhubarb fancier, but because it was served by our oldest friends in Alaska, I reluctantly accepted a piece of rhubarb cake. And then it happened. One bite of that cake was pure seduction. I ate two more pieces and lived to tell you the recipe.

5 cups rhubarb, cut into half-inch
    pieces
1 cup sugar
2 3-ounce packages strawberry
    Jell-O (or any red variety you
    like)
2 cups miniature marshmallows or
    large ones, quartered
1 package cake mix, yellow or
    white
Whipped cream

Grease a 9 x 13 x 2-inch baking pan. Spread the rhubarb over the bottom of the pan and sprinkle sugar over it. Now sprinkle Jell-O, right from the package, over the sugar and rhubarb. Then scatter marshmallows over the Jell-O.

Prepare the cake mix according to the instructions on the box and pour over the layers in the pan.

Bake at 350° for 55 minutes. Cool and serve with whipped cream.

CONCORD CRUSTLESS PIE

Knowing the problem I have making pie crust, someone devised a crustless pie for me and sent along the recipe. It is very rich. Arrange for help to eat it.

3 eggs
1 cup sugar
1/2 teaspoon baking powder
1 cup chopped pecans
3 tablespoons grated orange rind
1/4 cup graham cracker crumbs
1 teaspoon vanilla
Whipped cream

In a medium-sized bowl beat eggs until they are frothy. Add sugar and baking powder. Continue beating until thick and light. Add pecans, orange rind, crumbs and vanilla. Mix well and pour in a well-greased 9-inch pie pan.

Bake in a preheated 350° oven for 30 minutes. Remove to a cooling rack for 15 minutes and then chill until serving time.

Cut into 6 or 8 pieces and top with whipped cream.

YOUR JUST DESSERTS

CHAPTER
14

A heavy friend of mine I'll call "Al" is even bigger than I am. His favorite saying is, "Gordy, someday you'll get your just desserts." Usually, he makes the statement just after he's eaten a dish of mine that is packed full of sugary calories but tastes far too good to pass up. He tries to fill his voice with righteous anger. Fat or not, you must know how difficult that is when your taste buds are still lingering over a fantastic dessert.

One time, after a big helping of Blue Frog Farm Strawberry Jubilee, Al simply leaned back in his chair and sat there with a blank look on his face. Only his body was present. His mind apparently floated away on the gossamer wings of taste.

He sat so still for so long that I finally jabbed him with a fork to see if he was dead. He responded by pushing a clean-licked plate toward me and shouting, "Again!"

Oh, how he hated me the next morning, nursing a sugar hangover.

Just before Christmas last year I was invited to a dessert party. Eight of us showed up and there was food for twenty. I elected to try a piece of Heavenly Four-Layer Dessert.

The first mouthful was . . . well, to be honest, description is impossible. I'll try "delectable." When the lady who brought the dessert handed out recipes, I was among the first to grab a copy. I've made it at least ten times since that day. Yes, the recipe is in this chapter, but before you dash off to the kitchen to try it, it's time for a commercial for other cooks in my house besides me.

With but a few exceptions, in my opinion, only women make good pie crust. My three daughters, Laurie, Toni, and Pattie, and my granddaughter C.J. make the best pie crust in our family . . . I suspect, the best in many families. (No flaky comments, please.)

That commercial should earn me at least four large apple pies with excellent crusts. The girls can arrange delivery to my house anytime within a week of their reading this book. Or sooner.

My pie crusts do not always turn out tender and flaky. Maybe for Mother's recipe for chicken pot pie I'll have a go at making a crust, or I'll try a crust mix, but I even fouled one of those into a tough mess once.

For this reason, I welcome the new pie crust shells that have reached the supermarkets, and I suggest you use them for recipes in this chapter. Ask my daughters if you want pie crust recipes. And good luck!

My proofreader, the wife Connie, just mentioned to me that I have been referring to the term *mug-up* without explaining what a mug-up is to me. If you've read *LOWBUSH MOOSE*, you know, but for you who are just entering the world of Nelson cooking and Alaska lore, here is a brief explanation.

The term *mug-up* must have come to Alaska with the early sailors who visited the land. It was the first step in offering the hospitality of your ship — or home or camp or any other space you occupied. You offered the stranger or visitor a mug of whatever was available, coffee, tea, rum or other warming libation. The usual cold and wet condition of Alaska made the offer a welcome greeting.

Today offering a mug-up means that I'm offering a guest in my home a cup of coffee, or maybe wine, and whatever is freshly baked.

My own best-remembered mug-up goes way back. Dad and I were standing on a cold and windswept dock waiting for a ship. Then the cook aboard a cannery tender noticed us and leaned out his galley

"IS-IT-A-CAKE?" CAKE

My mother never said, "I can't make a cake because I'm out of. . . ." No matter what she was "out of," she could make something resembling cake. This recipe of hers calls for many ingredients, but if you're out of something, improvise.

1 cup apple juice, divided
1 cup pitted dates
1 cup raisins
2/3 cup shortening
1/2 teaspoon salt
1/4 teaspoon ground nutmeg
1 teaspoon ground cloves
1 teaspoon ground cinnamon
2 cups all-purpose flour
1/4 teaspoon baking powder
1-1/2 teaspoons baking soda
1/4 cup hot water
3/4 cup chopped nuts

Puree dates and 1/4 cup of apple juice in a blender. Pour into a saucepan and add raisins, shortening, salt, nutmeg, cloves, cinnamon and remaining apple juice. Simmer 3 or 4 minutes over medium heat. Cool to lukewarm.

Sift flour and baking powder together. Dissolve soda in hot water. Now add these ingredients and the nuts to the cooled fruit and mix well. Pour into a 9 x 13-inch nonstick baking pan. Bake in a preheated 350° oven about 40 minutes. Serve hot or cold.

This cake was a favorite in my lunch bucket.

ALASKA BLUEBERRY MOUNTAIN PIE

This is a variation of Baked Alaska that is easier both to afford and to make. It can be whipped up in record time to surprise a guest, or even a mother-in-law. Have a go at it.

1 quart slightly soft vanilla
      ice cream
1 9-inch pie crust, baked and
      chilled
1 21-ounce can blueberry pie filling
4 egg whites
1/2 cup sugar

Transfer the ice cream to the pie shell with a spoon and smooth it out. Add the blueberries to the top of the ice cream. Place pie in the freezer and freeze solid.

When the pie is frozen, begin the meringue by beating the egg whites until they are frothy. Sprinkle on the sugar, a tablespoon at a time, beating until the whites form stiff peaks. Spread the meringue over the pie, carefully sealing the edges.

Bake in a preheated 500° oven for 2 or 3 minutes, until the meringue is lightly brown.

Serve immediately!

BLUE FROG FARM STRAWBERRY JUBILEE

Since Blue Frog Farm has no cherry trees, making cherry jubilee is out. Last year, however, the strawberry patch came into its own and a recipe was born. Practice this one a couple of times, and then spring it on a dinner party.

1 quart strawberries
1 teaspoon cornstarch
1/2 cup brown sugar
2 tablespoons lime juice
1/4 cup rum
Ice cream

Pick out the best 3-1/2 cups of strawberries. Slice them and set to one side. Smash the remaining berries.

In a saucepan stir together the cornstarch and brown sugar. Add the crushed strawberries and the lime juice. Place the pan over low heat and stir until the mixture is bubbly. Remove from the heat.

Dish the ice cream into 6 dessert bowls and top with the sliced strawberries.

In a small saucepan pour the rum and light it with a match. Pour the flaming rum into the bubbly strawberry mixture while stirring constantly. When the flame dies, the sauce is ready to serve. Pour it evenly over the 6 dishes of strawberries and ice cream.

If you practice, you can perform the entire ceremony at the table using a chafing dish.

door, holding up a mug by the handle. This is the universal invitation to come aboard for a mug-up. His hospitality consisted of a seat by the roaring range and its welcome warmth, followed by coffee for Dad and chocolate for me. Oh yes, and his own warmth. I can still remember his grinning face, and that is fine enough immortality for any man.

The next most memorable mug-up of my life came as I moved into the teenage group and I began courting the local bootlegger's daughter. My hanging around the daughter had not met with her entire family's approval. Her father suspected my intentions, I'm sure. As a father of three now, I can better understand his thoughts, but to be honest, I didn't know what my intentions could be at the time mine were bothering him.

Her three brothers, Big, Bigger, and Biggest, didn't much care for me either. Only her mother smiled at me once in a while, a ray of sunshine.

Now let's give a name to the temporary girl of my dreams. How about "Kathy"? She was tall, full-figured and only fifteen.

One night after a Saturday dance, I walked her home. This was long before the automobile entered my life with its ready excuses for courting time, such as running out of gas, flat tires and so on. In those days one could claim, perhaps, that a pebble in the shoe made you walk slower — an excuse Kathy and I each used on the other sometimes to stretch the walking time to her house.

I don't recall if pebbles troubled us the evening of my next-most-memorable mug-up, but I do remember that the two miles to her house took us a very long time. As a result I didn't get my goodnight kiss on the front porch until 1:15 in the morning. She turned quickly and slipped into the house.

A fraction of a second later Biggest showed up at the end of the house, signaling "mug-up time." Since I was well over two miles from home and thirsty, I saw his offer as a kindness, maybe even the brotherly acceptance I sought.

We walked around to the screened-in back porch of the house where Big and Bigger sat at a table. As we came in sight, Big poured a mugful from a stone jug. When I sat down, he pushed it toward me.

I reached for the cup of what I thought would be apple cider with considerable pleasure, opened my mouth and poured a sizable slug of the liquid into me.

You're ahead of me, aren't you? And you're right, it was a cup of their dad's straight moonshine, aged one week. It went down my throat like a cat with all twenty claws extended and resisting being swallowed alive. Then it fell to the bottom of my stomach with a thud. I sat there a good five minutes, tight-lipped, watery-eyed and sweating.

My mind raced ahead to frightening thoughts of what the booze and/or the brothers might do to me. Then I began to feel the warmth in my stomach working its way through the rest of my body. The glow brought my arm up, lifting the mug for another swallow of liquid. It went down as smooth as silk, possibly because the first swallow had burned off every nerve-ending in my mouth and throat. Now I knew what the brothers meant by "smooth booze!"

By the time I finished the first mug of rotgut, I assumed I had three new friends, Big, Bigger, and Biggest. Now I realize they might have killed me with kindness and the stone jug except that by the time the second mugful was half gone, my stomach revolted. I made a run for the backyard to empty both containers, the cup and my stomach. I lay there on the ground for what seemed a long time.

I'm fairly sure Kathy had something to do with the next series of events. It seemed to be her voice my confused brain heard screaming angrily at her brothers. Then

there is a vague memory of my trying to walk and running into things. The fall into the creek on my way home, I remember well. Even in the summer it was cold. At home I stripped off my wet clothing and went right to sleep. I awoke ten hours later without a hangover. Ah! The resilience of youth.

Kathy, you ask? Sadly, our romance was over. A year later she married a guy with a cast-iron stomach. He was larger than Biggest, meaner than Bigger and smarter than Big. She was too tall for me anyway.

Let me add one small postscript, though. When I became a trooper years later, I had the duty to arrest Bigger for "drunk and disorderly" and Biggest for drunken driving. Would you believe, they accused me of arresting them deliberately to get even? It makes me smile, even now.

Most mug-ups of my life have been joyous occasions, and I hope the institution of mug-up hospitality never fades from the earth. Join in: work up any of the following recipes and signal a neighbor for a mug-up.

CHOW MEIN MUG-UP COOKIES

There are dozens of nice things to serve at mug-ups, but for a visitor with a sweet tooth, child or adult, this is a fine goodie.

12 ounces real chocolate chips
6 ounces butterscotch chips
1 cup chopped pecans
1 5-ounce can chow mein noodles

Place the chips, chocolate and butterscotch in the top of a double boiler and stir over hot water until melted.

Stir in the nuts and then the chow mein noodles.

Lift out as much as you can hold between 2 teaspoons and drop onto waxed paper. Repeat until you run out of mixture. At this point licking the pan is acceptable behavior.

Cool the cookies and serve.

Some variations: use different nuts; add a cup of tiny marshmallows to the mix; or use chunky peanut butter instead of butterscotch chips.

NELL'S CHERRY CHEESE PIE

I came home a month ago last Sunday riding a sugar high, a new recipe in hand. I sobered up the next morning and swore off sugar for two weeks. Then I weakened and made the wonderful pie myself.

1 8-ounce package cream cheese
1/2 cup sugar
2 cups whipped topping (Cool Whip type)
1 9-inch pie shell, baked and cooled
1 16-ounce can pie cherries with syrup

In a medium bowl whip the cream cheese until it's soft and mix in the sugar. Add the whipped topping and blend.

Turn the mixture into the pie shell, spreading it across the bottom and up the sides to form a cavity in the middle.

Add the cherries and their syrup carefully to the center of the pie and spread them out. Keep it neat! Chill the pie until it is firm before serving. Yield: 6 wedges.

HEAVENLY FOUR-LAYER DESSERT

This is the dessert I raved about earlier in the chapter. It is a real diet buster and I suffer sugar hangovers the day after eating it. That didn't stop me from making it six times last year.

Layer 1
Combine into a soft dough:
1 cup flour
1 cup pecans
1/2 cup melted butter

Press evenly over the bottom of a 9 x 13 x 2-inch baking pan. Bake at 350° for 20 minutes. Cool.

Layer 2
Cream together:
1 cup powdered sugar
8 ounces cream cheese
1/4 of a 13-ounce package Cool Whip

Spread this mixture over the first layer. Chill for 1-1/2 hours.

Layer 3
Mix well:
2 boxes (3.75 oz. each) instant lemon pudding
3 cups milk
1 teaspoon vanilla

Spread on top of the second layer and chill another hour until pudding is set.

Layer 4
Combine and spread over the third layer:
1/2 cup chopped pecans
1/3 more of the 13-ounce package of Cool Whip

Now you can serve this Heavenly Four-Layer Dessert. It is definitely "just desserts!"

CANNERY CURRIED FRUIT

I first tasted this dish in a cannery mess hall on Bristol Bay in Western Alaska. I had a bit of it hot for dessert one night, and some more, cold, for breakfast. It was good both ways. The recipe is large, but it usually sells well, both hot and cold. Take it to a potluck the first time you make it and let many people try it.

1 16-ounce can sliced cling peaches
1 16-ounce can peeled apricot
    halves
1 16- nce can pears, pieces and
    chunks
1 16-ounce can pineapple chunks
1/4 cup brown sugar
1 tablespoon curry powder

Open and drain the cans of fruit, reserving the juice. Place fruit in a casserole and mix well.

Combine half the juice with the sugar and curry powder and pour over the fruit.

Cover and bake at 350° for 1 hour. Serve either hot or cold.

YUKON GOLD RUSH BARS

This recipe came from my mother's files, so there are no dancing girls in these gold rush bars. The recipe is great for a large family; you can use up all the broken graham crackers the kids would otherwise fight over.

2-1/2 cups graham cracker crumbs
1 14-ounce can sweetened
    condensed milk
1 6-ounce package chocolate chip⌣
1 teaspoon vanilla
1 cup chopped nuts or raisins

This is a quicky. Combine all the ingredients in a bowl and mix well. Pour into a 9 x 9-inch square nonstick pan. Bake at 325° for 30 minutes.

Cool and cut into 16 chunks and stand out of the way of the oncoming kids.

SNOWDRIFT BOILED DINNER

A howling gale had been blowing out of the Matanuska River area for days, and the snow was drifted five feet deep. We were not going anywhere that day, but we still had to eat. This is what the cupboards and root cellar provided.

2 tablespoons vegetable oil
1 onion, halved and sliced
1 cup chopped green pepper or
    1/4 cup dried pepper flakes
1 12-ounce can corned beef, in
    1/2-inch dice
1 No. 2½ can (1 lb. 13 oz.) tomatoes
1 teaspoon salt
1/4 teaspoon rosemary, crumbled
1 teaspoon garlic powder
1 tablespoon dried parsley
1/8 teaspoon pepper
1 2-pound cabbage, cut in eighths

Put the vegetable oil into a Dutch oven over medium heat and sauté the onions and green peppers for 5 minutes.

Add to the pot 2 or 3 cubes of corned beef, for flavor, and all remaining ingredients *except cabbage*, plus water to cover. Bring to a boil and simmer 20 minutes. Add cabbage and more water, if necessary, to cover. Bring to boil again and simmer another 30 minutes, or longer, if cabbage requires additional cooking. During the last 5 minutes of cooking, add the remaining corned beef cubes and heat through. Serves 4.

CIRCLE CITY COOLER

When I last visited Circle, the community at the end of the Steese Highway on the banks of the Yukon River, it was 100° and the air was still as a rock. I had driven 100-odd miles from Fairbanks, sitting in a patrol-car oven in a wool uniform. With visions of a cool drink, I stopped at a small cafe, opened my parched mouth and whispered to the waitress, "Iced tea, please."

I received a blank look, so I added, "Something cold?" She was back in a minute with a 16-ounce glass of something that looked like muddy river water. Maybe a bit yellower. One gulp later I headed for the kitchen to beg for the recipe.

6 ripe bananas, mashed
12 ounces orange juice
12 ounces lemon juice
5 cups sugar
7 cups water (from a spring; not
    from the river!)
6 12-ounce cans lemon-and-lime
    soda

Combine bananas, juices, sugar and water. Mix well, pour into ice-cube trays and freeze.

When serving time comes, fill a tall glass with the frozen fruit cubes and fill in the spaces with ice-cold lemon-and-lime soda. Stir and serve.

Also try the cooler with 1-1/2 ounces of vodka between the cubes and soda.

GOTTA' TRIES

CHAPTER
15

Back in the good old days when my duties as a trooper sent me to and fro across the Great Land, I was always on the lookout for new recipes. A couple of my discoveries, a soup from a logging camp and a whitefish recipe from a fish camp near Iliamna Lake, I mentioned in my first cookbook.

Since the publication of that book, my active search for new recipes seems to be over. Instead they find *me*. Cooks everywhere, experts and beginners, seem compelled to help by sending along theirs. Some are family recipes which have been handed down for generations. Those I can "relate to," as you know.

The folks who give me their recipes verbally — in front of the meat counter at the supermarket, over the phone, in the middle of an intersection — flatter me most by their assumption that I know so much about cooking I can hear a recipe once and forever retain it in my head. I like to inspire such confidence, but, for the sake of

recipes I really want, I have to confess pen and paper are essential to my memory.

When people visiting my home try the verbal method, I quickly hand them writing tools. Usually that results in a short pause and a solemn promise to send me the recipe later. Sometimes I actually receive it, and it is nearly always worth the effort, theirs in the writing down, mine in the testing.

My incoming mail is the most enjoyable source of recipes because letters generally accompany them. Some — most, in fact — rave about the recipes and stories in my first book. A few point out a "typographical error" which they never blame on the author . . . like the woman who'd cooked up a gallon of very thin pea soup using my recipe. She *loved* the book but shouldn't the water in that recipe be listed in cups rather than quarts? She was so right, and I sat down at the typewriter immediately to tell her so.

Ninety percent of the recipes come with

POST OFFICE

notes that insist I "gotta' try!" them. I wish I could say I always do, but I cannot. I do read and compare all of them to recipes in my files and find many similar enough that testing is not really necessary.

Now and then, new and exciting recipes do come in and are greeted with pleasure. Sometimes, too, I am reminded of a seasoning idea I once knew and liked but had somehow forgotten. Using peanut butter as a flavoring agent in meat sauces and so on is an example of one welcome rediscovery that came to me in the mail.

Long before there was a cartoon named "Peanuts," I knew a man called Peanutbutter. I remember him partly because we shared a love of the sticky stuff.

My family was working out of Cordova at the time. I was aboard the cannery tender *Billy*, which my older brother commanded, and we were headed out on the Copper River Flats to buy fish.

Peanutbutter was the ship's cook, or rather he was the cook-deckhand-fishcounter. This was back in the 1930s, early Alaskan history.

Many of you do not remember the peanut butter of the thirties. It wasn't the homogenized kind we buy today. Instead it was a smooth oily stuff that smelled like peanuts. Open a jar, you'd find an inch of peanut oil floating on top of a rather hard glob of peanut concrete. The trick was to stir the oil back into the peanut butter and then eat it before it separated again. Otherwise the stuff in the bottom of the jar became harder and harder.

In fact there was a story going around that Ole Thompson had made an emergency patch on his boat's hull with a jar of peanut butter with the oil poured off.

ANIAK FRANKS
du JOUR

There are times in the cold, cold winters of Alaska when no one should go anywhere. On such a night I landed at Aniak, over on the Kuskokwim River. I walked in on some friends, with my sleeping bag under my arm.

The wife was standing on the back porch, looking into the Deep-freeze. I looked, too, and saw nothing except frankfurters.

"What do you do with them for encores when you've already boiled, baked, barbecued and casseroled them?" she asked.

I offered to cook the franks *du jour*. I used this recipe.

1 pound frankfurters, beef, chicken or whatever
4 ounces spicy brown mustard or regular mustard
4 ounces cranberry jelly, or currant, or . . . (you get the idea)

Slice the franks diagonally into 1-inch slices. Combine the jelly and mustard in a saucepan over low heat, stirring constantly. Add the frank slices and continue to stir while they heat.

Serve as the main course at dinner, or as a hot hors d'oeuvre at a party.

KODIAK
RUSSIAN TEA

During the time my family lived in Kodiak, my mother was fascinated with the Russian ideas and ways that are still alive from the days of the early settlers of the community. Making Russian tea was a serious business to her even though we did not use a samovar.

The ritual required a teakettle, boiling on the stove, and two teapots on the table. Let's go through the steps of making tea:

First, heat the number one pot by filling it with boiling water to the brim. When the pot is hot, dump the water.

Add to the warmed teapot 1 measured teaspoon of tea for each cup of water to be poured into it, plus an extra teaspoonful "for the pot."

Then refill the pot with boiling water and let it steep for exactly 4 minutes.

During the time lapse, *heat the second teapot with boiling water*, too. Empty that water and add to the pot 1 bay leaf, 1 whole clove, and a light pinch of thyme.

Now *strain the tea* from the first pot into the second pot and cover.

Serve at once and make a sweetener available. Mother always used currant jelly, 1 teaspoonful per cup.

GOTTA' TRY TURKEY

Is leftover turkey ever a problem at your house? If so, you'll like this recipe we picked up from the friends who gave us the recipe for rhubarb cake I raved about earlier. (Recipe, page 144.) Why not serve it for dessert to top off this stir-fried turkey?

*4 cups cooked turkey meat, cut in
    1-inch pieces
4 tablespoons vegetable oil
1 clove garlic, minced
1/4 cup soy sauce
1/4 teaspoon pepper
1 teaspoon sugar
1 cup chopped onion
1 green pepper, sliced thin
1 red pepper, sliced thin*

In a bowl large enough to handle it, combine the turkey and enough oil to coat it when stirred. Add garlic, soy sauce, pepper and sugar. Stir together and let marinate for 15 minutes.

In a large frying pan, lightly sauté onions and peppers in the remaining oil. Add the marinated meat and continue stir-frying until it is thoroughly warmed.

Serve as a main course, accompanied by a big bowl of noodles or rice. The dish will feed 6 to 8.

My first breakfast aboard the *Billy* consisted of a stack of hotcakes with a large gob of peanut butter in the middle. Yellow oil ran to the side of the plate and was soaked up by the cakes. I dove right in, smearing the peanut butter around and shoveling hotcakes in my mouth. The cook smiled at me.

Later that day, while we were at anchor with a dozen smaller boats around us delivering fish, I was busy handing out the free bread and the water hose. It was hungry work.

During a break in the action the cook handed out sandwiches and cocoa. Yes, peanut butter sandwiches. And for dinner that night we ate pork chops cooked with peanut butter. . . . Try Leona's Pork Chop Surprise, page 101, for a taste like it. It's a flavor you just "gotta' try!"

That same summer I received my first seal. No, not of approval, but a real live baby seal. All big brown eyes wrapped in cute.

One of the fishermen had captured the seal in his nets. Its mother had become entangled and drowned. He planned to knock the young one in the head but made the mistake of looking into its big wet brown eyes. He melted and managed to slip the seal to the skipper's kid brother when the skipper wasn't looking.

Ten minutes after the seal joined us, everyone in the crew, except the skipper, knew about it. When an hour later the entire crew was still gathered around a fish bin aft, the secret was out. The skipper shouted, "Throw it over the side!"

No one moved to comply. The skipper gave the wheel to the deckhand and marched back to commit the act himself. Leaning down to grasp the animal, he

KACHEMAK BAY SCRAPPLE

I first tasted this old favorite while sitting in a country kitchen overlooking beautiful Kachemak Bay at Homer on the Kenai Peninsula. Homer has always been a town with pleasant memories for me.

The plate I was served contained two large slices of scrapple, two eggs fried in butter and a half-dozen slices of yellow cling peaches. I had to have the recipe.

2 cups cooked meat, pork, beef,
*   ground beef or liver*
2 cups stock, beef or pork
3/4 cup corn meal
1 teaspoon salt
1/4 teaspoon sage

In a saucepan, over medium heat, bring the meat and the stock to a boil. Dampen the corn meal with a small amount of water and mix it into the boiling stock. Add salt and sage and continue stirring until the mixture thickens. Now pour into a 9 x 5-inch loaf pan and chill for 12 hours.

To serve, turn the loaf out onto a breadboard and cut slices about 1/2 to 3/4 inch thick. Fry the slices on both sides in a well-greased frying pan. Serve with eggs instead of toast. Or alone with butter and syrup. Or strawberry jam. . . .

ALASKA RUSSIAN POTATOES

No, we didn't get this recipe with the purchase of Alaska. Well, not as far as I know. Mine came to me by way of New York and Seattle. We merely added a few thoughts and claimed it for our own. You gotta' try.

3 eggs
1-1/4 cups milk
1 onion, minced
1 tablespoon flour
1 teaspoon salt
1/4 teaspoon pepper
2 tablespoons melted butter
8 medium-sized potatoes, washed
*   and grated*

In a large bowl beat the eggs, add milk, onion, flour, salt and pepper. Mix well and add the melted butter and grated potatoes. When mixed again pour into a buttered 2-quart casserole.

Bake in a preheated 350° oven for 1 hour or until the top is crusty brown.

Serves 4 to 6. Make cottage cheese or sour cream available as a side dish.

accidentally looked into those eyes. Oh! Those brown eyes!

The skipper's back straightened, and his eyes swept the worried crew. Then he spoke, "Can't you idiots see this animal is hungry? Feed it!" It was said firmly, as a skipper should speak, and then he stomped back to the wheelhouse.

For the next three hours, three men and a boy tried to find a way to feed a baby seal. A milk-sopped rag system seemed to work best, but it really didn't give him enough milk to keep him alive. It was suddenly evident to all of us that we were not going to be able to keep this tiny animal from starving. He needed a richer milk and a better delivery system than we could supply. Without his mother, he was doomed.

I sat on the box in the fish bin and petted the seal. Disconsolate, I started to eat the three-hundredth peanut butter sandwich of my young life. As I leaned down, petting the seal, some peanut oil ran down my finger. The small nose moved toward the smell and a small mouth caught the oil. Here was a fellow traveler, a peanut butter lover.

The cook opened a fresh jar of peanut butter and sacrificed a bit of the oil for a new formula for the baby. We mixed canned milk, a little water and the peanut oil. In another five minutes we had a solution to our feeding problem. We dangled the rag from the end of a bottleful of formula to act as a sort of wick. And the seal kept right on sucking the rag until the bottle was empty.

Naturally I wanted to keep the seal, but the local game warden knew about a zoo that wanted a harbor seal. His pitch finally convinced me the seal would be better off there.

The incident certainly demonstrated to me the benefits of peanut butter as a seasoning. In fact, you "gotta' try!" it for yourself.

While you're at it, you gotta' try these recipes, too.

PETERSBURG NON-CODFISH BALLS

As a young man living in Petersburg, I was exposed to the dish known as codfish balls, which I learned to enjoy.

Suddenly, forty years later, I'm snowbound nowhere near a cod, and I have an urge for codfish balls. That's when I invented Non-Codfish Balls.

1 egg, beaten
2 6-1/2-ounce cans tuna, drained
4 teaspoons minced onion
1-1/2 teaspoons lemon juice
1 teaspoon prepared mustard
1 cup bread crumbs

In a medium-sized bowl combine the egg, tuna, onion, lemon juice and mustard. Mix well and shape into balls of about 1-inch diameter. Roll the balls in cracker crumbs and fry in deep fat until golden brown. Keep warm until serving time.

GAS BOAT OVEN-BARBECUED LIVER

I was one of the lucky people born liking liver. Of course, those who hate it simply haven't tried liver that is cooked properly. This method, which I learned from a gas boat cook, is one proper way. Even liver-haters go back for seconds. It's definitely a "gotta' try!"

1 pound beef liver or pork, moose or
*   deer liver*
1/2 cup all-purpose flour
1 onion, sliced thick
4 slices bacon
1 cup of your favorite barbecue
*   sauce*

Start by rinsing the liver in water to remove the blood. Dry on paper toweling. Shake the pieces in a paper sack with the flour.

Arrange the liver slices in a nonstick baking pan. Place a slice of onion and a slice of bacon on each piece. Pour half the barbecue sauce over the meat and onion.

Bake in a 350° oven for 20 minutes. Then turn each stack over, making it bacon-side down. Pour the remaining barbecue sauce over all. Bake another 15 minutes.

Turn the stacks bacon-side up when dishing onto plates. Serves 2 born liver-eaters or 4 light eaters.

SUSITNA BAGGED SALMON

One of the most fascinating things about cooking is the constant opportunity to try new ideas alongside the old. Take, for instance, the plastic cooking bags now on the market. I've already tried most of the suggested uses for the bags.

One morning last week I eased a silver salmon out of the Deepfreeze and started planning a meal around it. The new bags popped into my mind, so I used one.

1 14 x 20-inch plastic cooking bag
*   with tie*
1 tablespoon flour
1 cup chopped onion
1/2 cup chopped celery
1/2 cup chopped green pepper
1 pan-dressed salmon (whole but
*   trimmed of head and tail)*
2 teaspoons salt
1/4 cup soy sauce
1 tablespoon lemon juice
Pepper

Start by opening the bag and throwing in the flour. Shake the bag to coat the inside with flour. Lay the bag in a 13 x 9 x 2-inch baking pan. Combine the onion, celery and green pepper in a bowl and then spread them across the bottom of the bag where the salmon is going to be.

Salt the salmon inside and out. Combine the soy sauce and lemon juice in a cup. Paint the salmon inside and out with this sauce. Pepper the fish and slide it carefully into the bag, laying it on the bed of vegetables. Add the rest of the soy sauce and lemon juice to the bag and tie securely. Poke 2 vent holes in the plastic bag.

Bake the fish at 350° for 2 hours.

At serving time, cut open the bag and slide the fish to a platter. I usually remove the top layer of skin and fat before taking the fish to the table. A large fish will serve many, with great leftovers.

By all means strain and save the fish stock in the bag and baking pan. Use it in soups and chowders.

WASILLA CHICKEN FETTUCINI

When my hostess at dinner one night announced the main course would be "Wasilla Chicken Fettucini," my taste buds prepared for a new and different treat, a real *spécialité de la maison*. As the dishes began to arrive at the table, however, they looked like "just noodles" to me.

I hasten to tell you how much looks can deceive! Or, as the old saying goes, you can't tell a noodle by its color. With the first mouthful of this delicious dish, I knew my taste buds were going to be rewarded after all. Yes, you gotta' try it.

4 quarts water
8 ounces green fettucini
3 tablespoons vegetable oil (olive oil preferred)
1 large onion, sliced thin
2 cloves garlic, minced
1/2 pound fresh mushrooms, sliced thin
1/4 cup butter
3 ounces ham, cut into julienne strips
1 teaspoon dried sweet basil, crumbled
1 large tomato, seeded and chopped
2 cups shredded cooked chicken
1/2 cup heavy cream
1/2 cup freshly chopped parsley
1/2 cup dry white wine
1/8 teaspoon ground nutmeg
Salt and pepper
Parmesan cheese, grated

Bring water to boil, add noodles and cook 8 to 10 minutes. Drain well. Butter lightly and set aside.

Heat the oil in a large skillet over medium heat and sauté onions and garlic until transparent. Add mushrooms and brown lightly. Mix in butter, ham, basil and tomato and simmer for 5 minutes. Then add chicken, cream, parsley, wine and nutmeg and heat through. Finally add noodles and toss gently to blend all ingredients. Salt and pepper to taste.

Divide the noodles onto 4 plates and pass grated Parmesan separately. Serves 4.

(Probably not)
THE LAST WORD

There are a couple hundred more recipes in my files and at least that many more stories in my memory about the good (and the bad), funny and sad times in my experiences with eating. I would like to present them all to you in this document. Alas, there isn't room.

Since the Alaska Nelsons — now four generations long and many more to come, we hope — have always liked eating and story-telling, especially when the two are associated, you will no doubt hear from us again. Meanwhile, I hope I've entertained you with these pictures of my family's life in the North. And have shared with you some very good times with food.

INDEX

SURE ENOUGH

Is NOT
The Last
Word

Sure enough, there's another book coming from the G. Nelson recipe file. While we printed *SMOKEHOUSE BEAR,* Gordy's been brewing Cookbook 3.

The title? We're not sure yet (though you're bound to recognize it). We do know it will include the story of how Gordy came to be dubbed "Tired Wolf" when his relentless pursuit of the recipes for good eating led him so often to "another man's kitchen." Just which delicacy was he after, anyhow — the cooking? Or the pretty cook?

Whatever his motive, Tired Wolf is not too tired to share in the upcoming book many more stories and recipes from the family, friends, pen pals and kitchens-afield you've come to know and love. Here's a few recipes to anticipate:

Pickled Postman Picnic Poppers. Spenard Barbecued Chicken. Seduction Steak. Kvichak Kabobs. Short Rib Sauerbraten. Alaskan Kohlrabi Soup. Kippered Apple Salad. English Bay Onions. Frying Pan Cake. Lover's Stew for Two. Out-a-sup Mustard Sauce. J.D. Chocolate Balls. Microwave Bagels.

If you'd like to be told when Cookbook 3 is available, send your name and address to:

Gordon Nelson Cookbook Club
Alaska Northwest Publishing Company
Box 4-EEE
Anchorage, Alaska 99509